CONTENTS

FORWARD

If you're reading this, it is because something compelled you to look beyond the surface. It is usually when we dig deeper, we find what most people consider treasure. Gold, precious metals, diamonds, gems of all kinds, sometimes food such as potatoes, peanuts, carrots, and others, and even more elemental, water, coal, and oil, all entice, feed, and provide life for our wants and needs above. Some are obviously more important than others from a survival standpoint. We must have water and food. It is not necessary for us, on a primitive level to have gold, gems, or even coal or oil, after all we can burn wood for cooking. However when you dig even deeper, you start to run into very hard rock and minerals, until you reach the very hot center of the earth, filled with molten magma. This is a place on earth, no man has ever been, yet we know it is there. There is evidence from time to time of molten lava rising from volcanoes in quite spectacular fashion, and we use this information to prove to ourselves the existence of the Earth's molten core. Sometimes these explosive volcanoes can destroy a beautiful snow capped mountain and leave behind a complete wilderness devoid of life, however, when you look a little closer, you start to see charred seed cones, that can only reproduce after being pried loose by high temperatures caused by a fire. These seeds start to grow in a rich environment of ash left behind by the fire that ensued. This wilderness, now starts very slowly to heal not in spite of the volcano instigated fire, but BECAUSE of it. The destruction was a necessary event, that would later reveal a stronger, just as beautiful in a different way, new growth.

Redemption of a beautiful forest from utter destruction, is a great example of resiliency and on a more spiritual level, endurance. The definition of endurance is "continuing existence." Isn't that part of the definition of life? Good things, bad, even tragic things that happen in life require endurance. It's not easy sometimes, and can seem insurmountable. You can dig a hole by yourself, but at some point, you are going to need help, either to dig deeper or to get out of the hole. You have made a decision to dig beyond the surface by reading this book and I want you to know, I have prayed for you. Perhaps this is the first time anyone has said a prayer for you. You don't have to be a believer to gain encouragement from my book, but I wrote this book from my perspective as a believer, and my prayer is for you to experience the transforming enduring love and support that believing in Christ gives. Knowing He was at first beside me, then healing me from the inside out, provided the miracle I needed to not just endure a tragic loss, but to grow beyond that loss into a thriving incredible new and better version.

ACKNOWLEDGMENTS

I would like to thank everyone who helped me with this book.
My beautiful wife, Shannon is a steady rock of support and
love who encourages me to honor God with only my best. My
Mom and Dad, who are the best parents anyone could ever
have. Jeremiah, for allowing me to be a part of your life. It is
an honor. My family. The many children I have taught music
to over the years, who unknowingly helped me recover, your
gift is still healing. Thank you Paul Deepan for your incredible
writing talent, and friendship. Thank you Bishop Choby for your
wisdom and love. I can feel your smile from heaven.
Thank you Paulette Carlson, for believing in me and allowing me
to accomplish a life long goal! Thank you Steve Freeman for your
support and prayers. Thanks to the many musicians I've had the
immense pleasure to make music with. Special thanks to Terri
Morris with Mollie B. Creative for the artwork on my book. You
are an incredible artist, but more importantly an encouraging
friend in Christ. Special thanks to my attorney John Prince
for his steadfast and knowledgeable support in all my creative
endeavors.

Most importantly, thank you Jesus, for everything, especially
allowing me to wake up in the morning after that life changing
event. I hope sharing this story gives you the glory you deserve,
and a lot of new friends.

A prayer we would pray in school before each music class…

Dear Lord Jesus, thank you for your gift of music.
We ask that you bless us with it, so that we may use it
to bless you and to help those who may need it.

In the name of the Father, Son, and Holy Spirit

Amen

Chapter 1

THY WILL BE DONE

Have you ever achieved your lifelong dreams, only to have them come crashing down around your head? This exactly is what happened to me. Then, amazingly, God gave me an amazing second chance to live a different life, and find abundance beyond my wildest dreams.

I came to Nashville, Tennessee, known the world over as Music City, as a young man from a small town in North Carolina, with my heart set on making it in the music business. But just like thousands of other young men and women before and after me, life in the music industry didn't go exactly as planned.

In one way, I carved out a life that many outside of the music world would find enviable. I became a guitar player in a band that toured all over the world, playing for tens of thousands of fans. I became first the road manager, then the artist manager, for the performer who played in front of these fans. Next, I became a manager for other, well-known artists, negotiating record deals and concert appearances with promoters in the United States and Europe.

However one day, when I was 37 years old, I suffered a catastrophic medical event, most likely caused by the misguided prescription of a blood pressure medicine. My brain was deprived of oxygen, leaving me with symptoms similar to those seen in people who have suffered a massive stroke. Overnight, I forgot everything I knew about playing my music. I also lost the ability to follow a simple conversation, let alone negotiate the nuances of a European tour.

Suddenly, I'd become a shadow of my former self. And, I felt the classic emotions of people who have suffered an actual stroke: anger, fear, and shame. In addition to the loss of my career in the music industry, my personal life unraveled over time. Believe me, it would have been easy to give up. But somehow, behind the frustration of losing my musical ability, a lot of my memory, and other cognitive abilities, I had the unshakable feeling that God would somehow lead me back to a place where I could once again share my musical talent with the world.

You see, despite my fairly rapid rise up the corporate ladder of the music industry, I feel in retrospect that I had not been putting my musical gift to work in the world the way that God had intended. To be sure, I was making my full-time living within the music industry, and felt lucky to do so. I'm very aware that this does not pan out for most people who come to Nashville. I didn't do drugs or abuse alcohol. I didn't sleep around or cheat on my wife when I was married. I always conducted my business dealings with integrity. So I never viewed what happened to me as a punishment, and never believed that this catastrophic event was a mark of God's displeasure.

I had always viewed God through the eyes of a child, believing without question His grace and goodness. One of the things that my event did to me was rob me of the "executive function" that most adults have. In other words, it reduced me in some ways to the mental state of a child, which in turn reinforced that child-like approach to God. With that child-like vision, I always believed that God would return my musical abilities to me. My new job, therefore, became figuring out how to do His will, and not my own.

Today, nearly 25 years after the event that robbed me of everything I had worked so hard to achieve, I think I'm *finally* learning how to do that. I've seen the points in my life where God was trying to get my attention, and I wasn't listening. First He whispers, then He touches your face softly, then He nudges you, then He smacks you! Since that event, I have learned how to pay better attention to Him. God has returned my musical abilities better than they were before. I have also been blessed with creative insights, involving areas of science where I've had no formal education. These insights have allowed me to invent products that help others, while enjoying more abundance in my life than I've had for some time.

I don't think I would have been able to do all this without finally learning how to surrender to God's will for me. I'm not saying that everyone who has a stroke will be blessed by a return to normal simply through an increase in faith. That would be trivializing the pain, shame, anger and fear, which many stroke victims feel. I have known those feelings all too well. But when I speak about "faith," I don't just mean belief in God, but trust in God. I do believe that this aspect of faith (surrendering to God's plan, rather than always trying to force your own) can help everyone, no matter where they are in life, or how "successful" they think they are.

I've had worldly success. I also know first-hand how quickly it can leave you, and how fast you can disappear from people's lives once they don't think you can help them anymore. What I have now is so much more valuable than what I had then, even though most of the world might not agree.

Perhaps you or a loved one has had a catastrophic event (whether a stroke or something else entirely), which has turned your life upside down, and someone has suggested you read this book. If so, then I hope reading my story will help you write your own story, one with a different ending than you can imagine today.

Perhaps you are very successful, but are beginning to feel that empty space where that elusive "something more" might be hiding. Finally, perhaps you've had some hard knocks, and are just looking for some light in a very dark place. Either way, you might be looking to take a different turn in your path through your life.

I hope that by sharing my story with you, I might be able to help you find the path you are looking for, or maybe even one you haven't thought of yet. I believe God's talking to all of us, and if we take the time to listen and accept His invitation, troubles might not disappear, but He will give us the ability of a "mustard seed" to handle anything.

Will you walk with me for a little while?

Chapter 2

WHISPERS
Here We Come...

If you head east on Interstate 40 out of Nashville, Tennessee, you will eventually reach the foothills of the Appalachian Mountains. The countryside becomes more folded, with steep hills and valleys, interspersed with grassy plateaus. There's a lot of history along this drive, even more if you take the time to venture onto some of the secondary roads.

After a few hours, you'll pass through Knoxville, Tennessee, and eventually the edge of the Great Smoky Mountains National Park, which straddles both Tennessee and my home state of North Carolina. Once in North Carolina, there are a couple of ways you could choose, depending on how much of a hurry you are in, to get to my hometown of Gastonia, just west of Charlotte.

When I was little, Gastonia was a medium-sized town. When I visit it today, I find it hasn't changed much in some ways. I will say it has grown over the years, and is now close to the Greater Charlotte area. One of the best things about Gastonia is how unique the food was, and is. There's a place called R.O.'s Barbecue, and I suspect that everyone from around Gastonia will know about R.O.'s. They have a barbecue slaw that's more like a dip, and which has a distinctive taste: I've never tasted anything like it anywhere else. Some of our relatives who still live there will still send us some of that unique slaw at the holidays.

Because it is relatively close to the ocean, Gastonia has a large number of seafood restaurants, known locally as "fish camps," where you can get awesome seafood. Another fond memory I have of Gastonia is a place called Tony's Ice Cream, on Franklin Boulevard. Tony's is a family-owned place, which has been in business since 1915. They boast 28 flavors of ice cream, which they make next door in their own plant.

Gastonia is also noteworthy for the relatively high number of professional athletes and coaches it has produced, in baseball, football, basketball, and NASCAR. I guess I'm proud to come from a little town that has produced so many talented folks.

Gastonia had a couple of drive-in theaters, which don't exist anymore. Some of my musical experiences took place in those drive-ins when I was really young, and my parents would take me to the drive-in to see a new Elvis movie.

There is a main strip, and later on, when I was in high school, we used to cruise up and down that strip, the same as any other teenagers in many other small towns in America. I have a lot of fond memories of doing that, and I'd say, all in all, that I have many good memories of Gastonia.

I was born in Gastonia on January 14, 1960, at the dawn of a new decade. And what a decade it was! The 60's were arguably one of the most tumultuous in history that didn't involve a major global war. There was Martin Luther King and the civil rights movement, John and Robert Kennedy, Marilyn Monroe, the Vietnam War, the Apollo moon landing, and so much more!

And then, of course, there was the music.

If you believe, as I do, that music is magical, then some extra special magic was happening during that turbulent decade. As a little kid, I was insulated from a lot of the big ugly conflicts that happened in the sixties. It was the music, and the memory of that wonderful music, that seeped into the consciousness of those of us who were little kids in the sixties, but didn't come of age until the seventies.

My earliest musical memory is of jumping up and down in my Mama's car singing to the radio at the top of my lungs when I was three years old. Yes, once upon a time there were no seatbelt laws! Even then, I think I felt the strongest of emotions, a sense of belonging, whenever and wherever music was playing, a connection deep within my soul that has never left me and has only become stronger with time.

I suppose I had a pretty normal childhood. Although I was an only child, we had family who lived nearby. These were just regular folks from the point of view of what everybody tended to do in those times in that place. Fortunately both my parents are still alive and they live right next door to me in Springfield, Tennessee! I know that might not be everybody's ideal living arrangement, but I think it's pretty cool, especially given some of the help I needed after the "stroke."

My folks moved out to Tennessee about five or six years after I did. I guess they saw that I was going to stay here, especially after I became somewhat successful in the music business, and they wanted to be closer.

My mother was the second youngest of nine kids in her family. (And no, my mom and dad were not Roman Catholics, although I became one later in life!) Because my Mom was younger than most of her siblings, the majority of my cousins were quite a bit older than me.

My grandmother, whose first husband died, was married twice, so my Mom and my Aunt Jenny were half sisters. I remember Aunt Jenny's daughter, my cousin Suzy, would babysit me. There was a pole in Aunt Jenny's basement, which I would climb up and slide down, and pretend I was Batman (from the corny TV show that was popular at that time).

Suzy had three brothers: Sam, Butch and Ronnie. Butch was also quite a bit older, and he had red hair and loved to hunt rabbit and fish. I suppose I hero-worshipped Butch a little, as you do with your older male family members. I remember my Dad and Butch used to love to go rabbit hunting. Butch would come over to the house when I was about four or five, and my dad and he would walk into the woods down Long Creek to go fishing. I would cry because they wouldn't take me, and I idolized Butch.

I feel that Butch and I always had a connection. When I got old enough, I finally got to go rabbit hunting with him and his dogs. I remember one day when we were hunting down in eastern North Carolina, his dogs jumped a rabbit, which they had chased down into the holler ("hollow" for non-Southerners). The rabbit began circling back, and I could hear Butch and the dogs coming up. I prepared to shoot and just as that rabbit jumped in the air I nailed him with a shotgun. But just as I lifted my gun to shoot I heard Butch holler: "Don't shoot my dog!" I killed the rabbit with a good clean shot while he was in midair. No harm came to the dog, and I guess Butch trusted me after that.

It's always good to trust that your hunting partner can kill the game without shooting the dogs (or you, for that matter!)

While hunting was fun, music was always my passion. By the time I was 5 or 6, I already knew I wanted to play the guitar. I remember my grandpa playing his guitar with my great uncle, Clyde Reynolds, who played banjo. (I still have my Grandpa's guitar, and have recorded with it in recording sessions). Clyde was my dad's uncle, and ran a TV repair store. Grandpa and Clyde would sit outside, either on the porch, or in the shade of the pin oak trees, and play. Next door to my grandparents lived my Aunt Reida. Her husband Tom played Chet Atkins-style electric guitar. I was mesmerized by his finger picking and would be influenced by it later when I started to play guitar myself.

I also remember when my cousin Ronnie (Sam, Butch, and Suzy's brother), would play rock music on the electric guitar, and how exciting that sound was to me. So looking back, I can see that even though my Mom and Dad weren't musicians, I was surrounded by a lot of family members who loved to play. I believe they reinforced my own love of music, and gave it a lot of room to breathe and grow,

In those days, music was also still very much a part of a public school curriculum. I had my first musical performance in first grade at Costner Elementary School, on the triangle. It was at the Dallas Auditorium in Dallas, North Carolina. Our class played rhythm instruments, and everyone who performed had to wear a uniform. I remember feeling like I belonged on stage. I also recall, from the same performance, some older students playing the theme from The *Monkees* TV show, the one that begins: "Here we come…" I was completely mesmerized watching those older kids play and believe, even though I couldn't put it into words then, that their performance touched the musical part of my soul.

I've wondered sometimes if that's what an addiction must be like, because I just couldn't get enough.

I wasn't shy about letting people know that I wanted to play guitar, and in the second grade, when I was seven years old, I received my first one. This was a Sears Silvertone F-hole acoustic guitar, which I still have today. (An f-hole guitar is one that has two holes, not a single big round one.) This particular instrument came with a blue tinted foldout instruction sheet on how to play the guitar.

I spent hours and hours with that blue sheet, trying to teach myself for several years, with limited success. My parents were finally able to find the right guitar teacher for me when I was in the fifth grade, aged 11. My first guitar teacher was a wonderful lady named Miss Michaels, who was 90 years old. She was a great teacher who was younger than her years, and had two pet iguanas.

Miss Michaels was the first one to cultivate my gift and has remained a lasting inner presence throughout my career. She was very patient with me and seemed to know that I had a natural aptitude for music. Even though I loved music so much, there were still times when I might not practice a piece as much as I should. Miss Michaels always very gently made me want to do better when those situations arose.

One day, Miss Michaels paid me the huge compliment of telling my dad that she didn't have anything left to teach me, that I needed to find a new and more accomplished teacher than she was. I did go to another place to take lessons, but I've never forgotten Miss Michaels and her iguanas.

At age 12, my soon-to-be band director, Mr. Sterling P. Woodard, brought the junior high concert band to play for my elementary school where he was recruiting for future players. Of course I was really interested! When he asked what I wanted to play, I couldn't think of the instrument's name, so I said, "You know, that thing Louis Armstrong plays!" I had heard Louis sing and play *Hello Dolly*. Like so many people, I thought Louis Armstrong on the trumpet was one of the coolest sounds I've ever heard. I began playing trumpet in the seventh grade. By the next year, I was first chair and had a solo at the junior high school during our spring concert.

I still don't know if I was especially gifted, or simply more committed, than other kids my age when it came to music. Whatever the reason, by this time I was never one of those kids that you had to force to practice. The feeling I most recall is one of total amazement at being allowed to do something I loved so much. I literally could not get enough of music. We tend to think of Commitment as a word that denotes a lot of hard work. But when you love something as much as I love music, the time you spend with it doesn't feel at all like work. What felt like work was time spent doing anything else. I wondered why anyone had to take pesky subjects like Math and English!

My solo was *Rainy Days and Mondays* by the Carpenters. Mr. Woodard directed me with the William C. Friday Junior High band. I must have done something right, because the following fall he asked me to march in the high school marching band. This was at North Gaston High School, where he was also the band director. I was still in Junior High and so short that my Mom had to take my pants up to the knees! I must have looked awkward marching in such an outsized, and weirdly altered suit, but I didn't care. Being in the band just fed my need for more music. I was always so excited to play during the home football games and some away games. I was by far the youngest musician on the bus trips, and was probably something of a mascot to the older kids.

I'd also been fortunate that my parents loved music, and although they weren't musicians themselves they did like to go to concerts, often bringing me with them. During my childhood, my parents took me to some country music concerts and to two Elvis concerts. I remember seeing Grandpa Jones, Tammy Wynette and George Jones when I was little. Ironically, I would meet two of them when I later became part of the music scene in Nashville.

Elvis was at the height of his fame at this point, so you can imagine the excitement in the crowd before, during, and after his performances! I distinctly remember, after one of Elvis' concerts, as we were driving away from the Charlotte Coliseum, I turned to my folks and said, very simply, that one day I too would be playing in Coliseums full of people. Children can say the most prophetic things. That was a goal that solidified in my mind, and was, in fact, something I would later accomplish.

In 1973, I got my first electric guitar as a Christmas present, a Fender Telecaster, with a Fender Deluxe Reverb amp, (both of which I still own.) By age 14, my guitar and I were playing rock, country, and R&B music with other kids at each other's homes. I learned how to play *Johnny B. Goode*, by the amazing Chuck Berry, when I was 14 or 15 years old. The 70's were a great time to learn to play music. There were all of those great songs from the 50's, 60's, and 70's, up until about 1974, when disco came on the scene. It seemed as if there were artists churning out great new music for a budding musician to learn, on an almost daily basis.

My dad and I would sometimes visit music stores on Saturdays, and one, called Carroll's Music Store (in Ranlo, North Carolina) was particularly notable. Carroll was the owner and an excellent jazz guitar picker. At any given time, you could find Carroll in his store leading jam sessions with other musicians. One day there

was no bass player and he shoved a bass in my hands
and told me to follow along. I was scared to death, but I gave it
my best shot and I think I might have hit every other note along
with a few sour ones, but it didn't matter, the fact he invited me
to pick with them was a moment of feeling like
I was one of them, "a musician," however lacking in experience I
might have been.

Later on, there was another notable music store in The Gaston
Mall: "Buddy Lee Music." Buddy Lee, the owner, picked the
banjo and guitar. One day when my dad and I were at his store,
Buddy Lee showed me a common country lick based on an
arpeggio. It was an eye-opening lesson for me, and I still utilize
that technique to this day. I learned a lot about the craft of
improvising by hanging out in music stores with such talented
musicians. You never knew who might be there any given day.
It was exciting for me!

During these early teen years, I was still going to church
regularly. My folks were Presbyterians and our church had a
youth group. The adult church members were very supportive
of our youth, and people knew I could play. They really wanted
me to play with them for a Christmas play, and it would seem
natural that I would want to use that additional opportunity
to play music and perform. But despite my desire to play in
front of thousands of screaming fans like Elvis, I was very shy,
even squeamish, when it came to playing music with only a few
other musicians, especially in church.

I did press through my shyness, and helped them with one
Christmas concert, but that was it. Although they really tried to
persuade me otherwise, and were very encouraging, I just didn't
feel that playing in church was for me.

I only did that one performance with the youth, and I've thought a lot about this decision over the years. I believe it might have been the first time I may not have listened to God whispering in my ear when it came to my music. I think that my shyness might have played a role, but this shyness disappeared later on when I played in a rock/pop band at school. In a weird way, I think I felt unworthy to play "for God."

I also think I may have had some rigid ideas about God, and whom he deemed worthy. Church seemed so special to me that I felt somehow inferior around other people in that circle. Even though the band was about more than me, and my guitar, I felt self-conscious about receiving accolades for performance when God was supposed to be the one being worshipped.

I also had some pretty rigid ideas about the direction I wanted my music to take. Like the 60's, the 70's was also a decade where young people continued to push the envelope of authority, and music was definitely one of the tools that we used to push against that envelope. Playing popular music was a little rebellious and edgy. Playing in a church youth band was not, and didn't fit the image I was creating for myself. It simply didn't have enough of a "cool factor" for me at that time. So, given the "noise" that goes on in the head of every adolescent, and the noise being made by all the changes in society, I found it easy to ignore that first whisper of an invitation from God, asking me to use my gift for His purpose.

When I was 16, I started taking piano lessons. I think this was an influence from one of my aunts (Barbara, another of my mom's sisters), who played. I loved to hear Aunt Barbara play *Sleigh Ride*. I was fortunate to be learning three instruments at the same time: trumpet, guitar, and piano. This diversity really helped me understand music better, as well as become a more versatile musician.

In high school, Mr. Woodard created a class for a jazz band, but in reality we were a pop rock group with a class time during school to practice. For kids who love music this was awesome. We had two guitarists, a keyboardist, and a trombone player, with trumpet, bass, and drums. We played at basketball games, and gave concerts at school. The very first time I performed on TV was at a Belmont Abbey basketball game. Of course we thought we were really big-time and very cool.

During my junior year of high school, our jazz band was asked to give a concert in the auditorium. We decided to create some special effects, beginning with buckets of dry ice producing lots of fog behind closed curtains. We dramatically opened the curtains to our opening song: *Fire*, by the R&B/Funk band The Ohio Players. When the curtains opened, it looked great and our fellow students in the audience loved it.

For the middle of the song, we had rigged up some homemade flash pots. As we couldn't find any flash powder, we used gunpowder instead. I was very careful and told our drummer the exact amount to use. But of course the drummer (being a drummer) thought it would look even better if there was a little *more* powder to give things a little more bang for the buck. Unbeknownst to us, he took it upon himself to add more. I learned the very important lesson to never let a drummer loose with gunpowder for a stage performance!

When we set off these jerry-rigged, overloaded gunpowder pots in the middle of our song, not only could we feel the heat on stage but the first four rows of the audience looked as if they had witnessed an atomic explosion! Unfortunately the principal of the school, Mr. McClure, was also seated in the first row. Yes, we all got called into the office the next day. Mr. McClure scolded us about the danger in which we had put the school and our fellow students. He also warned that if I ever pulled another stunt like that I would really regret it. He explicitly told me: "I am going to hurt you if you ever do something like that again!"

I did say in our defense that I had been very specific about the amount of gunpowder to use, and hadn't meant any defiance or disrespect, but I wouldn't say who had decided to use more. But Mr. McClure viewed me as the leader of the band, so I took the heat, if you'll pardon the expression.

Those noisy 70's was also the decade where the downstream consequences of the civil rights movement began to unfold, against the backdrop of the Vietnam War. I really loved playing and being mentored by Mr. Woodard and was very fortunate to have had him as my band director all the way through Junior High and High School.

I mention some of this historical backdrop because it just so happened that Mr. Woodard was African-American. I don't know, in retrospect, how much pressure he may have felt being a black faculty member in a predominantly all-white school. I don't remember hearing anything derogatory about him or directed his way, but that doesn't mean it wasn't happening in subtle ways. To me, Mr. Woodard was the really cool mentor who introduced traditionally "black music" into the musical repertoire of a white school. He even had us dancing to these tunes when we played them for football games and parades. We were definitely the coolest high school band around.

But I do recall Mr. Woodard being very stressed by holding down the jobs of both middle school and high school band director, and who knows what else. I specifically recall one day when he became so emotional on the football field that my dad went up to console him.

Perhaps my musical leadership in high school led Mr. McClure to bring me into his office in my senior year, and ask me whether I thought Mr. Woodard would be better as a middle school or high school band director. At first I told him that I couldn't really choose, because I'd had him in both places, and it was difficult for me to think about him along the divisions of Junior High vs. High School. At the time, I didn't realize how inappropriate it was for him to have this conversation, and I was also naïve to the potential political ramifications of my opinion. So when Mr. McClure kept the pressure on, I answered that because Mr. Woodard was so good at developing musical skills in younger kids, he would be an excellent middle school band director.

It turned out subsequently that after I had left for college the school decided to take away Mr. Woodard's position as the high school band director. Knowing what I know now, this meant that he lost the ability to select talent for the showpiece band, which is always the high school band.

This was probably why, after several years when I went back to see Mr. Woodard, and thank him for all he had done for me, he was very cold and essentially shut his door in my face. It seems pretty clear, in retrospect, that my comments may have been taken out of context and used as ammunition to rob Mr. Woodard of a position that helped enlarge his stature. To this day, I feel badly about my possible unwitting role in hurting someone who had brought so much joy to me.

I didn't know about any of this at the time, though, and generally speaking I loved high school. This was mostly because for three straight years I was not only given permission, but also actively encouraged, to hone my skills as a musician. And since I was so in love with music, it would be hard to contemplate a happier life. At graduation I was fortunate to receive the John Philip Sousa Band Award* by Mr. Woodard, and was also voted Most Outstanding in Music by my fellow students. I was also the president of the band that final year.

For my Christmas present in my senior year, my parents also bought me a banjo. I remember picking it up and almost immediately figuring out *Foggy Mountain Breakdown*. Although I didn't really pick up the banjo again until my second year in college, my fourth instrument had entered my life.

---

* "The John Philip Sousa Band Award is the pinnacle of achievement for high school band students. Created in 1955, it is an optional award given by the band director to honor the top student in a high school band and is limited to one student per school per year to recognize superior musicianship, loyalty, cooperation, and dedication."

(Source: ww.dws.org)

Chapter 3

CARESSES
Small Fish, Big Pond

As many freshmen have experienced, my first year in college required a significant adjustment in attitude, at a number of levels. As a senior in my high school, I was first chair in trumpet, leader of the jazz band, president of the school band, winner of the national Sousa award, and a big fish in a small pond.

But in my first year at East Carolina University, in Greenville, North Carolina, I was suddenly and unceremoniously... not so much!! While I'd been enjoying success at every musical level back in Gastonia, I had not really understood the scope of musical talent and level of instruction in other, larger, talent pools. I had unknowingly succumbed to the temptation of complacency. When I arrived at Greenville I encountered other students just as talented as I was, some even more so.

Although I worked hard, I was behind in music theory, my playing technique, and other performance aspects. I soon found myself depressed regarding my musical abilities. This was very unfamiliar territory for someone to whom music had always come so naturally, and for whom it had always been so joyful.

To make matters worse, my professor changed the mouthpiece size on my trumpet, (which flung my higher range into the basement), all in the name of "improving tone," which was something I thought I already had! My general studies were also suffering. I recall pulling at least one all-nighter to finish a term paper. I felt as if this wonderful place to learn music, where I had arrived with such excitement and anticipation, was attacking me on all fronts.

I was emotionally raw and ready to admit I'd made a big mistake. In stark contrast to the enthusiasm with which I had arrived, I now wanted to quit the program. I had just about come to this decision one morning, when I had a long phone conversation with my Dad. He shared words of encouragement with me that I carry to this day.

During our conversation, I beat myself up pretty badly, and probably said some stupid things like I didn't deserve the space I took up on the earth, etc. Today, as a father myself, I know it must have hurt my dad to hear me say such things, but he didn't react in a dramatic way. Instead, he was a pillar of quiet strength to me. He reminded me of all the good times that I'd had back home: "Remember what it's like to catch trout up in the South Mountains?" and, "So what if you fail a class in school, it's not the end of the world is it?" Getting permission to fail, especially from a parent, took a big load off my mind. Whether I passed or failed, I realized that as long as I did my best I wouldn't disappoint my folks or myself.

Perhaps most importantly and practically, my Dad encouraged me to go back to the trumpet mouthpiece I had been using. When I told him I didn't think I could do that, he asked me why my professor had changed it. I said, "to give me a better tone." Then he asked if my tone was in fact better, and I said,

"Well, no, it's way worse." So he said, "Well do it anyway, and if you sound better than you've been sounding maybe your professor won't mind so much."

Now most students considered this professor to be difficult, and many didn't care for him much. But I really liked him. I think he liked me as well, because although he wasn't too happy at first that I had returned to my original mouthpiece, he couldn't deny that I sounded a lot better. He let me keep to the original, and I could hear the improvement in my playing. This helped everything else, and life became a little easier after that.

The twin realizations that it was OK to fail, and important to stand up for what you believe in, were very important lessons for me to learn. I owe my Dad a lot for helping me learn them.

Instead of quitting, I decided to become the person I needed to be to succeed in my new circumstances. Armed with this new attitude, I began practicing in a field near the Tar River, which flows through Greenville about five blocks from the edge of campus. I would go out there and practice a little, and play a lot. Instead of three walls and a door, there were Live Oaks draped with Spanish moss, muscadine vines, and pine trees surrounding me when I practiced. It was very relaxing. This was a place where I cried out to God, both with my voice and my horn. It is difficult to describe, but it was in this place, during these solo musical interludes, that I felt His presence and found His peace. This peace came not only through the beauty of His creation, which surrounded me, but also through the understanding that music was God's personal gift to me. This was the first time I consciously felt God's desire for me to use my gift for Him.

Although I did finally make it through my freshman year at college, it wasn't easy. By the time I got back home to Gastonia at the end of that year, my confidence in my ability to play the trumpet was still shaken. I needed something to restore my faith in my musical ability. This came in the form of my very good friend Russell Smith, who had been my best friend in high school, and who lived about half a mile down the road from me. Russell had one of those assertive but likable personalities to which it's impossible to say "No."

Russell did no more but drag me down to Myrtle Beach with him, where there was a cable TV show being broadcast from the Hilton Hotel. Essentially the gentleman who did the show would find local talent to play his broadcasts. He would stay at the beach for the summer, then head up into the mountains in the fall and broadcast from the ski resorts. Russell went up to him and promoted his (as-yet non-existent) "amazing bluegrass group," which included me playing banjo. The host actually put us on! My buddies had to push me to do this, but with their support I got the break from the trumpet I needed and affirmation from playing and having fun again. In this way, a lot of my confidence returned.

Because I had a great summer, when I began my sophomore year this confidence returned to school with me. I also made new friends who would become blessings for me, both personally and professionally. Buoyed by this new sense of optimism, music and my studies were fun again. Life was good. Have you ever noticed that it can feel easier to turn to God when life is miserable, than when it's going well? I hadn't forgotten feeling God's presence on the Tar River when I was so low. It was more, that since life was easier again, I felt that He'd answered my prayers, so I was good to go. Again, I'd learn differently, but not until quite a bit later on.

One of my classmates in my sophomore year was a sax major called Dave Powers. I met Dave while auditioning for the jazz band at ECU. We already had a jazz connection because I was a trumpet major. Another guitar player was also at the audition, so I asked him if I could see his guitar. He let me play it, and I began playing riffs from a Doobie Brothers song. This immediately caused Dave to say that he played guitar as well.

Anyhow, Dave and I hit it off, and he came to the dorm room to jam. When he saw my banjo leaning against the wall he asked if I could play it. I hadn't really played my banjo much yet, as you may recall. I said I knew two songs, and we jammed. It was fun, and, just like that, I had a new friend. As an aside, that's the power music has to connect people in a deep way on a very brief acquaintance.

Sometime in the late fall or early winter of my sophomore year, Carowinds Theme Park in Charlotte advertised auditions for their music shows. The auditions were to be held at the East Carolina campus, which was convenient. Our professors said that anytime we had an opportunity to audition we should, so we did. Dave and I played *Foggy Mountain Breakdown*. They asked us to play another song, so we did, which was the only other song we knew! To our very pleasant surprise, we were given a callback audition in Charlotte, North Carolina. We auditioned again and afterwards found ourselves being measured for costumes. They said they would call sometime in the spring if we made it.

We had only auditioned for the experience, but I did receive a phone call. As it turned out, we weren't selected to play at Carowinds, but we were invited to play in Cincinnati, Ohio, at Kings Island Amusement Park! As you might expect, we took that gig! We performed that summer in Cincinnati at what would become our first real professional gig. It was six shows a day, six days a week. If you've read Malcolm Gladwell's book, *Outliers*, you'll know he talks about the amount of intense practice it takes to become really good at something. The musical example he used was about when the Beatles played in Hamburg, doing a ridiculous number of shows a week.

Looking back, I can see that my summer in Cincinnati was like the Beatles' Hamburg. There's nothing like having to play 36 live shows a week to make you really good with your instrument! I felt at the time that it was God's way of redeeming my hard work and answering my prayers to Him during those days on the Tar River. It was without a doubt one of the most exciting times of my young career.

During that summer, we also performed on a variety show in Cincinnati called *The Bob Braun Show*, televised to over two million homes. Before we returned to school, Dave and I also performed at home plate of a baseball game where we thought maybe 4,000 people would show up. After we finished our rendition of *Dueling Banjos*, the announcer came on and stated that: "tonight's attendance was 17,500 people!" We nearly fainted.

By the end of that summer, things were going really well for me. So when another invitation from God arrived, suggesting I put my musical gift to work for His purposes, once again, I wasn't really listening.

After we returned for our Junior Year, Dave and I continued to play together. In the late fall we got invited to hear a top-40 Christian band play for a Youth Rally (to help bring kids to Christ) somewhere in eastern North Carolina. We were told to "bring your guitars and be ready to perform," so I brought my

12-string. I remember one of the songs we played was *Roll Away the Stone*.

I remember thinking, "this music is cheesy." As a musician with a God-given talent I remember thinking, "this is not doing the music justice; it is not doing Jesus justice." I often felt guilty about that, because I'd felt, "maybe I'm supposed to be playing this kind of music," but I just couldn't do it.

Looking back now, I believe this was a maturing process I had to go through. However, I also knew that I felt, even then, that sometimes there are musicians who say they are performing for God in the name of God, but who are not authentic. I did not want to be a part of that. There were, and are, many who glorify God through their talents, but I just wanted to be authentic and true to myself.

I thought, and still believe, that such an explicit attempt to connect with young people generated music that felt forced, even insincere. It felt fake to me somehow. At the Youth Rally, besides *Roll Away the Stone*, Dave and I played a lot of popular song tunes, with rewritten "Christian" lyrics. Playing deliberately "sanitized" rock tunes in that atmosphere just didn't work for me. I've never been a fan of re-writing songs. Doing so to target an audience, especially one that you feel you might lose otherwise, has always felt exploitative to me.

However, before I ride away into the sunset on my high horse of musical purity, I should also mention something else. Despite continuing an active prayer life, my prayers were becoming more and more about ME, and my desires, and not about me AND God. I wasn't asking how I could fulfill HIS desires for me. I'm not saying that a secular career in music is a bad thing. It's not. I wanted one. I had one. I'm just saying that

I don't think a secular career was EVERYTHING God wanted me to have.

By this time in my life, I was imagining myself as a "successful" guitar player/ songwriter, with "success" measured by the benchmarks of how the world measured such things: albums sold, concert tours, and posters hanging in kids' rooms. Although I was asking for God's help, my plans pretty much didn't include glorifying Him with my music. I hadn't yet really understood that playing music for God was in one way as successful as you can be as a musician. The world didn't and doesn't see it that way, and I'd guess that most of my young fellow musicians in the early 1980s didn't see it that way either.

I could only define success in one way: I needed to get a band, write songs, then magically one day a record label would take us on, sign us up, and then: Boom! We'd be up and running. This is the myth and the fairytale that all young musicians tell themselves: "I can make the jump."

Today, with the Internet and advances in online connectivity and technology, it is possible to gain a very decent following as a musician even without a record company putting you on their label, or even going on tour. However, in the early 1980s, record companies still ruled the world. It was no wonder that I felt in order to be successful I had to go down the same road that everybody else was traveling.

Our own self-judgment and self-talk can be the biggest obstacles to us having the most intimate relationship available with God. This is because of the way in which they lead us to create our own images of ourselves, rather than the image of ourselves that God has of us. Unfortunately, just like being self-conscious about playing music, we can become overly self-conscious about being with God. The truth is, "you don't feel comfortable with it until you feel comfortable with it," and sometimes it can take a pretty serious wake-up call for you to get there. However, at this stage of my life I wasn't mature enough for such deep reflection. Life was going along pretty well, and there didn't seem to be any urgency about thinking along these lines.

During my junior year Dave and I and another music student started a top-40 cover band, called *Rumour*, with two other local musicians who were not attending school. Dave played keyboard and the saxophone; I played the guitar, trumpet, and banjo. Our fellow student Woody, who was a trombone major at ECU, played the bass. Our drummer was a really great guy called Tim Tyson, who worked for a living. Our singer Jim, who also had a "real job," was the person who had advertised for the band, because he wanted to form one.

Because of the several different instruments we could each play, we could perform pop, country, bluegrass, rock, and rhythm and blues. We played anything from *Dueling Banjos* to Pink Floyd's *The Wall* in our set list. We played wherever there was a bar willing to hire us. One of our favorite towns was Jacksonville, North Carolina, where the Marine Base Camp Lejeune is located.

I played in *Rumour* from about halfway through my junior year through graduation. One night we were playing a nightclub and our singer Jim, who was a very large man in excess of 350 pounds, had jumped down from the stage to the dance floor to dance with the crowd during my guitar solo. If you can imagine Meatloaf dancing in the crowd you might get the idea. Anyhow, when Jim ran to jump back onto the stage, which was only around 5 inches high, the toe of his shoe just barely caught the edge of the stage, and he began to fall. It seemed to take an eternity for him to finish falling! As he fell, he landed against the cymbal stands, and they swayed back and forth as sweat flew in seeming slow motion up into the air.

When Jim finally came to rest, the rest of us were laughing so hard we nearly stopped playing. What made it even funnier was the song we were playing was *Hurts so Good*, by John Mellencamp. Somehow we managed to finish the song. But we immediately took a break and went to the break room, where Jim, who had a really strong Georgia accent, said: "I could've been killed and all y'all could do was laugh!"

I said, "If you'd seen yourself you'd still be laughing too!" I would pay $1,000 to see a video of all this, but unfortunately this was before the era of smart phones. Of course, playing in bars there were a lot more stories like that I could tell, but the main reason to mention *Rumour* is that it gave me another opportunity to hone my performing skills, which would again help me later when I moved to Nashville.

Time passed, and the end of my college career came in sight. My official major at ECU was Music Education. A lot of musicians take this route, as a fallback in case their performing career doesn't pan out. The other usual option is Music Performance. To secure my Education credits in my last year at ECU, I was supposed to do a semester of student teaching. At that time teaching was one of the most difficult things I had ever tried to do. I was certainly not very good at it. I could help children learn their instruments pretty well if I worked with them one-on-one, but when teaching formally in front of a group, I was an absolute failure. I was told by my observing professor that I should never teach, which was a difficult position to be in if I wanted to graduate with a degree in Music Education!

My professor was going to fail me, but I made a deal with her that I would not teach if she would pass me. This presented a bit of a dilemma to the school, because I didn't have the prerequisites necessary to graduate with a major in Musical Performance, and I sure wasn't going to get the teaching credit I needed to graduate in Music Education!

As it turned out, this teacher worked with the appropriate authorities so that my degree simply reads Bachelor of Music, with no area of concentration. I have reflected on this situation many times, as it is one of many moments I believe God used to redeem me. It also became a very ironic wrinkle in my life later on. As they say, if you don't think God has a sense of humor, just make a plan.

On a brighter note, after years of work, my senior recital on the trumpet went really well. I made my trumpet professor proud, using the mouthpiece he had originally wanted me to put aside.

Chapter 4

NUDGES
Hit the Road, Jack

One of the recurring themes in this story is listening to God. That's not always an inner voice; God can also say hello in the form of other people whom He brings into your life at certain times, and those with whom He allows relationships to end. A lot of these relationship transitions happened during the years 1983-1985.

As you may know, musicians have a bit of a reputation for the shenanigans they get up to when they are on the road (!) But I had lived a pretty sheltered life as a small-town boy from Gastonia, North Carolina, so I wasn't really into too much of the wild stuff. However, one night, while I was still at ECU, *Rumour* was playing a gig in Jacksonville, and I met the girl who became my first wife. Her name was Denise.

Denise lived on the coast of North Carolina, which is a beautiful place. I met her there playing a Marine bar (as in, a bar for members of the U.S. Marine Corps). It was full of these very tough Marines every weekend, but they were a good crowd.

Then, shortly after I graduated college in 1983, the band *Rumour* broke up. Essentially, my friend Dave, Woody the bass player, and the drummer Tim decided that they wanted to play more than we had been doing. They wanted to play what we called the "Holiday Inn Circuit," which meant going and staying in a hotel for a week and playing a gig in that town for the entire week, coming back home doing some laundry and heading out for another gig the next week.

I was a little hurt, because my friend Dave was one of the leaders behind this decision, but did not invite me to join them. In one way, he probably did me a favor, but you know what it's like when you aren't asked to the dance.

In any event, I found myself looking for a gig and was lucky to do so with Nicky Harris, a recording artist based in Greenville right where ECU and I were located at the time. I had a full-time job with Nicky and learned a lot from him about performing. I enjoyed my time with him immensely and Nicky and I soon became good friends.

Denise and I were also married in 1983, after I finished college and gotten the gig with Nicky.

Denise and I had a lot of fun the first couple of years we were married. I also had a great time working with Nicky and touring with him on the road. By 1985, Nicky had developed enough material to record a new album. He traveled to Nashville, to record with one of Elvis Presley's longtime producers. He asked if I wanted to go, and having seen all those Elvis movies back in Gastonia and having gone to see Elvis twice in concert I said, "Yes of course!" It was amazing to listen to Elvis' producer tell some wonderful stories about his time with "The King."

It was also very powerful to watch amazingly talented session musicians work their recording magic in a professional studio. I still remember the smell the recording tape made while laying down tracks! This is, sadly, an analog sense memory lost to our digital world.

After Nicky took me to Nashville to record with him, I fell in love with the town. I just knew this is where I was supposed to be. Of course, I probably romanticized Nashville, as you do when you visit the place where so many of your heroes and legends got their start, or became famous, or both.

However, my desire to move to Nashville did also make sense from a career development perspective. As a musician, if you wanted to take your career to the next level, you were going to have to move to a place that would let you do that. Nashville, especially if you are from the South, is the most logical place for you to go. I mean it's not called Music City for nothing! So the idea of moving to Nashville had been in the back of my mind for some time, even before I'd finished school, and after that visit there with Nicky, I knew I wanted to move there.

Nicky had been able to carve out an artistic career without coming to Nashville (due to certain family responsibilities, which he took very seriously), but this was very rare, and he knew it. So he was very supportive when the musicians who worked for him felt it was time to take that step.

As it happened, Denise had a girlfriend, who in turn was very good friends with Leland Rogers, (Country Megastar) Kenny Rogers' brother. Leland had produced *The Gambler* movie for Kenny. While on the road with Nicky in 1985, I met Leland on Kenny's tour bus at the Hampton Arena in Virginia. Leland gave me an autographed photo of Kenny and his mother, which

I still have in my studio. Knowing my plans, Leland told me when I "got moved to Nashville," to call him. When Kenny was performing there, he said, he would take care of me.

This was all tremendously exciting, except that, unfortunately, Denise did not want to make the move to Nashville. The seeds of the end of our marriage were sown over this disagreement.

There are always three sides to every marriage story: his side, her side, and the truth. I don't want this story to be a "tell-all," so I think it's important to stick to the facts as I recall them. Denise was a decent person. She worked hard, which I really respected. But when I came back from Nashville, after that fateful trip with Nicky in 1985, and told her we needed to move there so I could further my music career, things started to unravel.

I'd always been clear about my intention to move someday. When it looked like becoming a reality, Denise made it clear that she didn't want to go. For one thing, she probably felt very insecure about leaving her Mom, with whom she was very close. For another, I know now that there are a lot of folks who come from small communities who have no desire to explore beyond the place they've always lived. Denise may have been one of these people. Nashville might just have scared the heck out of her, but all I could see was opportunity.

However, after a lot of back and forth, we did make the move, Denise wanted me to promise that we would stay for two years, and if nothing happened, we would move back. And I told her very honestly that I couldn't promise that, but we finally made the move in 1987. As it happened, after two years things were in fact just starting to happen. But Denise said, "Well, I'm ready to move back," and I said, "Well, you'll be moving back by yourself, then, because I'm not going."

I suppose I was being stubborn. I must admit I can be, sometimes. Even though I don't recall agreeing to a two-year limit, it may also be that Denise's definition of "something happening" may have been different from mine. In any event I was finally beginning to see some opportunities, pathways I could follow to make my dreams come true. I simply could not abandon those dreams at that crucial point.

One silver lining amongst this tension was that after we got to town, I did call Leland. He left backstage passes for me to which I met both he and Kenny before the show. During the show Leland sat me next to his wife in the front row. This is one of those moments where God was giving me a glimpse of what was to come. The opening act for Kenny at Starwood Amphitheatre was none other than *Highway 101*! I had no idea that in just a few short years I would be playing guitar and managing Paulette Carlson, who was then the lead singer for *Highway 101*, and, as an added twist, we would be the opening act for Kenny Rogers. Leland had given me some great advice when I came to Nashville. He said: "Take whatever job that will get you in the door for music and do it to the very best of your ability." That advice would later solidify my career. God is great!

Anyhow, after the fateful two years had passed, Denise had begun talking to her mother on the phone a lot. She got herself wound up and apparently decided that I didn't really care. It's true I was really busy, holding down a full-time job while trying to catch a break with my music. From where Denise was sitting, it may well have seemed that she was sitting pretty low on my "priority totem pole."

Then Denise had a brief affair, which I heard about second-hand from her best friend, who came up from Florida.

Apparently it was "only" a one-night stand. Denise came in the door, trying to patch things up. I wasn't interested. I said, "Look, you know, you're going to have to go back to North Carolina, I'm staying here." So that's how things went down. It would make a decent country music song, now that I think about it, but it was hurtful at the time, for both of us.

Denise and I were married from 1983 to 1990. We had moved to Nashville in 1987. The ironic thing was, just about the time my marriage ended, things began to really move on the music side, but not, as they say, without having paid my dues. The bill for my progress included my marriage, no matter whose fault that was.

For a place that is so friendly on the surface, Nashville can be a very tough city, especially when it comes to the music business. I had arrived in town armed with a music degree (albeit without a major!), professional ability on four instruments, and a lifelong passion for music. Like so many bright-eyed musicians before me who had come to town, I believed that with enough hard work, I could turn those attributes into a career writing songs and performing.

But dreams don't pay the rent or put food on the table. Like most musicians who come to town I had to find a "real" job. I was very blessed to find a job that not only paid well, but also gave me a real world education in business management and marketing. This hands-on experience became invaluable to me as my music career evolved.

When we first moved to town, I found work at a food brokerage called Heldman Brokerage, which represented Sara Lee® and Ragu® and other familiar brands.

Mr. Heldman was an interesting guy. He had been a Vanderbilt basketball star, although he was an older man by this time, of course. Gosh he was a penny pincher! But he was also one of the best salesmen I've ever seen in my life, before or since. There's a grocery chain headquartered in Cincinnati called Kroger's, who have many stores in Tennessee. He could go into almost any Kroger in his territory, and you could tell they loved him there.

On the other hand, the people who worked for him had mixed feelings about him, because he squeezed his money's worth out of you! But I learned a lot from him; a lot of things one should do, in terms of selling, and a lot of things not to do. I told him that the day I left, and he didn't like hearing it much I guess. I wasn't saying it in a mean way; I just said it as a fact.

At that time, there were a lot of different grocery chains such as: H.G. Hill, Food Lion, Kroger's etc.. What the various food manufacturers would do (instead of hiring folks themselves to represent their products in every store to make sure it was on the shelf), would be to hire a broker, with its own sales force, to do that.

A food broker would represent different products for different manufacturers, to different grocery chains, as long as they weren't in competition with each other. (For example, a broker couldn't represent both Ragu and Prego). They would pay the broker a percentage per case sold. They would run their deals through the brokers, and the brokers' sales people would present them to Kroger's, H.G. Hill, all the different stores. The conversation would go along the lines of: "If you buy this many cases, we can give them to you at this price," and then with that discount the stores could sell it at the regular price if they wanted to, or have a sale themselves.

As I mentioned, Mr. Heldman was a real penny-pincher, and at first I wasn't making enough money. One day, a friend of mine, who played with me in a top 40 band in town, and who worked for Coke, told me, "Hey man, you could make good money doing this," so I said, "OK, I'll try it," and I went to work for Coke.

This ended up being even a tougher gig! I had to be there at 5 am, driving a big truck (the tractor part was as big as a semi with a modified trailer). I had to start over by Old Hickory Blvd. and Nolensville Rd. My route was from that Wal-Mart over there, all the way down to Chapel Hill. I had to cover that every single day. If you know the Nashville area, you'll appreciate what a big geography that is.

First thing each day, I'd have to unload a hundred cases at the Wal-Mart, and build those huge multi-case displays in the stores. By the time I got to only the second stop, I was already pretty tired.

It took me too long to do it, as I couldn't bring the truck back until 8 or 9 o'clock at night. Then I'd go home, and do it all again the next day. After only about two weeks, I'd had a bellyful of that. I called in sick at Coke, and walked in to Mr. Heldman's, office, to which he said, "What are you doing here?" I said, "Well, I'm back at work now, for you." He replied, "What do you mean? You're working for Coke now." I could tell he'd decided to have some fun at my expense.

I said, "Well, I'm just gonna sit here all day long, until you give me an assignment." He replied, "Well "I don't believe you." Things went on like that for a little bit, until I said: "Well how many things can I do to annoy you today?"

I began playing his game, which was really unlike me. But I really wanted my job back. To be honest, I knew if I could get back in there, I could get a better one later.

So finally, after about an hour, he said, "I'll tell you what: You go out there and you sell, just like you sold me just now." I replied, "Well I want a raise, and I want to be a supervisor." He said, "You can be a supervisor, but I ain't givin' you a raise!"

He hired me back. That was my first lesson in not taking no for an answer, which stood me in good stead when I had future conversations with hard-nosed record label executives.

Meanwhile, I hadn't forgotten my original dream of breaking into music (which is another reason why hauling cases of Coke from 5 am to 9 pm wasn't going to work). Not long after I had first come to town, I had met a gentleman by the name of Al Cooley. Al was in charge of MCA's catalog for writers. He gave me some good advice when I first went in there. I have to admit I was nervous. This guy was from New York, and brash - not at all like other New Yorkers (!)

I had co-written a couple of songs with a couple of guys. I had written one by myself, and we'd recorded them. Mr. Cooley let me play the songs for him, listening to the first few seconds of each one.

He asked: "Who wrote these two songs here?" And I answered, "Well, this one was me and this guy, and this one was me and another guy." Mr. Cooley asked: "Who wrote this one?" And I replied, "Well, I did." He said, "Well that's the best one, you need to get rid of those guys and write by yourself."

He gave me the number of NSAI, the Nashville Songwriters Association International. He said: "You need to go here, and these folks will help you with your craft." He was really complimenting me on my potential to be a writer. This was the dream I had come to town with, but dreams can have surprising endings.

I'll never forget Al as long as I live, and he comes into this story again.

As I'd predicted, after going back to Mr. Heldman, in 1990 I did secure a better job with another food broker, a new outfit called PL Marketing. Instead of partnering with specific food brands and selling them across all stores, they sold only within Kroger stores. They represented all the Kroger-branded products in a Kroger store. (These are the "generic" products that carry the Kroger logo on them, sold within Kroger's as the house brands). PL Marketing was started by executives from Kroger's, in Cincinnati, one of whom, a man named Pete Tucci, had come down to Nashville to hire.

I was Pete's first Nashville hire. It turned out that this job was a good step up for me. I was in charge of the entire Kroger marketing area based in Nashville, which extended east to Knoxville, north to the middle of Kentucky, and south down to Huntsville, Alabama. This was a big territory for one guy, but it was a good job: I had a company car, expense account, and made good money.

This time, when I left for PL Marketing, Mr. Heldman wasn't upset, like you might think. He may have thought my move benefited him, because he would have contacts. But he may also have had my self-interest in mind, because he told me: "I usually tell a man when he screws up, and when he's doing the right thing. When you went to Coke, that wasn't a good move, but you're doing the right thing this time." He was really very gracious about it.

When I went to work for PL Marketing, I learned a lot about numbers, and how the Kroger business model worked. For example, I learned that manufacturers paid slotting fees to have their products on the shelf, so part of my job was to maximize the shelf space where they would be displayed, both to increase revenue for my company, and my own commission.

Again, PL Marketing only sold Kroger brand products within Kroger stores, but the company had to market their own branded products to store managers, as they were very autonomous at this time. The Kroger store in Green Hills was a great example, and ended up as one of my biggest success stories. When I went in there to talk to the manager I said, "Listen: you don't have enough Kroger products on your shelves in here." She replied, "I'm in Green Hills, Darlin'. Ain't nobody gonna buy that Kroger house label stuff over here."

You see, Green Hills is a pretty affluent part of town, so she was basically telling me that generic brands wouldn't have any appeal to her upper class clientele. I said, "Well, I tell you what, here's what I'll do: you let me put in 30 items, and we'll track them. I'll bet you dinner at Ruth's Chris that your sales will increase. Not only that, your profit margins will be bigger."

She said, "It'll never happen!" I mean, she was shaking her head, and clearly didn't believe it was possible. But Ruth's Chris is a really nice steak house, so she gave in to that temptation, and agreed to my experiment in her store.

When we ran her numbers two months later, she came up to me and hugged me. She said to me: "You have made my store number 1 because of those items! And so now I want you to put every single Kroger item you have on my shelves."

So that just goes to show you how Kroger's needed people to help represent their products, even to their own stores, because the managers had so much autonomy at the time. Even the people who were supposedly in charge of the brand at a local level might not necessarily believe in it.

The reason for sharing this piece of my journey is that all of that real world business training and experience really helped me. You see, most musicians don't have a clue about business, but I did. I really got a great education in marketing, sales, keeping track of profitability (so that I could get paid too), and negotiating deals and contracts. As you can imagine, this really helped me later on in selling records, especially when dealing with promoters.

In 1991, after I'd been at PL Marketing about a year, my "Big Opportunity" arrived. Life was never the same afterwards, for both good and bad.

Nashville is a music town, of course. A lot of folks who come to town, like I did, want to break into the music business. Although it is very competitive, musicians are generally a supportive group, and will often help each other out if the help isn't going to create direct competition for gigs. As it turned out, a friend of mine, who lived across the hall from me in my apartment complex, was also a guitar player by the name of Damon Medic. He was the road manager for an artist named Paulette Carlson.

Paulette had been the lead performer, and founding member for the band *Highway 101*, whom I'd seen courtesy of Leland Rogers when I was still new in town. *Highway 101* had enjoyed decent success with concerts and records, but, as is often the case, differing internal priorities caused conflict within that band. The end result was that Paulette was no longer involved. Paulette was a really good singer, guitar player, and songwriter. She felt, rightly so, that she was talented enough to try a solo career, which is what she was doing around that time. In 1991 she released her first album, Love Goes On, and was touring and developing material for a second album.

Damon and I had written a song together, and he appreciated my knowledge of the guitar. At that time he was looking for a guitar tech for Paulette's shows. He hired me for that job, because he thought it would be a good opportunity for me. It was. A guitar tech is the person who takes care of all the guitars when the band plays, tuning them and restringing them as necessary. Players often want new strings every other gig (some artists like them every single gig). The tech will unload the guitars, get them in tune prior to a set, and pack them back up ready for transport at the end of the show. If anything goes wrong with the guitar, the tech fixes it, as well as the equipment (e.g. amplifiers and whatever else people have on stage). The tech is kind of a cross between an equipment manager and tech support, and really needs to be on his/her toes during a show.

There are a couple of challenges to being an instrument technician for a touring band. One is: if you would like to be thought of as a player of that instrument yourself, you need to be careful about being thought of merely as the "guitar tech," and not as a "player." In other words, the risk is, if people see you schlepping the instruments around and setting them up, they can begin to discount your aptitude and talent on the instrument itself.

The other issue is, you need to be at the shows where the band is playing, which means you are on the road with them. The problem with that is that the job doesn't pay very much. If you have a pretty decent day job, and the guitar tech job isn't paying enough to leave it completely, scheduling time between going on the road with the band and fulfilling your responsibilities to your employer outside of the music business can become challenging.

Fortunately, my boss was a really nice fellow. He worked with my schedule and let me take off early. Because most of Paulette's work was on the weekends at first, when I traveled with her I wasn't shirking my responsibilities at PL Marketing. Plus, I was making money with both PL Marketing, and with Paulette, so I was doing pretty well financially.

Damon was Paulette's road manager. The road manager is not the same as the artist manager, although one person can fill both roles. The road manager is responsible for the logistics of travel, the bus rentals, managing the bus drivers, and the hotel rooms. He deals with the promoters to get all the info ahead of time, such as where the bus is headed and the location of the venue.

On our very first out of town gig, in Ocean City, Maryland, Paulette did something that I will never forget. She had taken the guitar off her strap, onstage, and was about to switch to another one that was all set up for her on a stand, also onstage. I was standing over in the wings, realizing that I needed to get the guitar she'd just taken off, when all of a sudden she just tossed that guitar at me! She wasn't upset with the instrument or me, it was just like a spontaneous thing, where she just tossed it at me to catch it, so she could put the next one she needed on her strap. Thankfully I caught it, but I was a little freaked out: it was a very nice Gibson guitar!

It just really frightened me because I would never do that with one of my own guitars! I guess because I didn't drop it, Paulette believed in me. This ritual became a little signature thing between Paulette and me ever after. It became part of the show. I suppose we developed this strong sense of trust pretty early because of that. In addition, we all traveled together on the bus, back and forth between all these gigs. The road is when you talk and really get to know one another. Paulette was always very good to me that way, and we developed a strong professional bond.

After I had been doing this for a little while, my friend Damon unfortunately messed up his position as road manager. The most important part of the road manger's job is to take care of the artist. This means: a) getting her to the venue, and b) making sure she gets paid. All the other musicians would be at the venue early, but Paulette, being the star, would often arrive later, getting ready and mentally preparing for the show. The road manager would arrange this separate transport. After the show he would also pick up the check.

That second part was where Damon eventually messed up. He was a bit of a ladies' man (unlike anybody else in the music industry). One time, he got involved with a lady, and forgot to pick up a check from a venue that we'd played. You just don't do that! Apart from the hit in cash flow that a delayed payment can make to a touring band, that kind of mistake can really raise red flags about how seriously someone is taking their job. Unfortunately for Damon, not long after that he was let go.

If this were a Hollywood movie, this would be the point where the star would turn to me and say: "I'd like you to be my Road Manager, John," but it didn't happen quite that way. Although I was developing a very good relationship with Paulette, she still didn't know me that well. So instead of coming directly to me, she hired another guy as the road manager, which was totally fine with me, as being a road manager was not a job I was interested in. I did care about Paulette well enough by now to have a concern for her welfare, and really felt the new road manager was a shady guy. He was also very abrasive and mean. I didn't feel it was a good thing for Paulette's career to have this guy representing her.

It wasn't long before my assessment of this guy's character proved to be correct. He started stirring up all kinds of trouble with the band. He even got quite mean with me one time. Remember, I was still only a guitar tech at the time and therefore pretty low on the totem pole.

One night, there was a conflict with a promoter. In his management of the situation this road manager said one thing to the promoter, and an entirely different thing to Paulette, within both earshot of myself, and the band. The promoter was pretty mad, and Paulette felt as if she had to defend her road manager. However, she didn't know all the information. When I saw that the truth was not coming out, and that she was going to look foolish going to the wall for this guy, I spoke up. I said: "Listen, this guy's not going to do any good for your career. He's pissing off more people than he's pleasing, and he's not helping you."

I went through the whole story with Paulette, telling her what we had heard him say, not wanting his job, or anything like that. I didn't want to be a road manager; I still wanted to be a musician. Though I still was not playing yet. After I had that meeting with Paulette, I had to have another meeting with her and her husband, Randy. And I sat down with them, and told the same story.

About two weeks later I got a phone call from Paulette. I was still working at PL Marketing and Paulette said, "John, Randy and I would like for you to come over to dinner tonight." So I said OK, and went over to the apartment she stayed in when she was in town. (She had a house, but it was way out in the country somewhere). When I arrived, Paulette said, "Randy and I were talking, and we'd like you to consider being the road manager."

I was honestly taken aback by this, but I said, "Really?" and realized I was honored they thought of me this way. I said, "Well, I would do that, tell me what I need to do, first though!" (Don't forget I'd never done the job itself), and Paulette told me, and so I said: "OK, yeah, I might be able to do that."

Of course then I had to call my boss at PL Marketing. I told him: "Look, I don't know how long I'll be able to make this work, you know, having both these jobs." But he told me, "We'll hang with it for a little while," I guess he was thinking that like a lot of music gigs it might not have worked out. He was probably protecting me.

I continued to do both jobs, and I actually enjoyed it, because I was in charge of all that stuff. I had all the airline tickets, for instance, when the band had to fly. I remember the first time I let all the band members have them and when we got to the airport to go to the next town, I said, "Does everybody have their ticket?" And one guy (of course) says, "I can't find it!" And I said: "You can't be serious!" And so after that point I made a new rule, I figured that one out quickly, and I said, "OK everybody, when we land at the next airport, all the tickets come back to me!"

So that's what they did: I took them and put them in my briefcase, and from that point on it was never an issue. But that was a classic example of learning on the go.

Being Paulette's Road Manager was a good time, though it could be stressful. My biggest anxiety about being the road manager was that I was always worried about safety. For instance if Paulette was getting on stage in the dark, I made sure people had lights and were getting ready to hold her, because she was wearing stiletto boots.

I remember one day there was this lady deputy sheriff back near where our bus was parked. I had asked a couple of times for more security near the bus, but there was nothing. I'd gotten to the point where I was aggravated and I was reading this poor deputy the riot act. I was saying things like: "Look you know I have my artist here, what happens if someone comes on the bus uninvited? This is ridiculous!" So that's how I was talking to her, and finally I left her and she had assured me that things would get taken care of. I went back on the bus to take care of some other paperwork, and realized Paulette had been on the bus the whole time and could hear every word I'd said to that poor deputy. I didn't know Paulette was there; otherwise, I might have tried to be nicer! But Paulette came up to me and, really softly, said: "John you can't be so rough on those deputies!" It was one of those funny moments like "Oh okay," and you feel sheepish, but it was also one of one of those moments when you realize your artist doesn't really need to know about all the stuff that has to happen properly in order for the show to go on.

I loved all of it though. At some point after that, we were in Los Angeles, and Paulette and I were shopping on Sunset Strip. Have you ever been on Sunset Strip? You know what it was then? It was a stripper's paradise, so this whole place was nothing but these little X-rated joints, and it was a little strange to be there with Paulette, who to someone looking on would have been this cute little Midwestern woman looking in these stores.

They sold this particular kind of little *bustier* that she wore with her dress when she performed, which was why we found ourselves there. Paulette would go in those places to get it. Of course, I, being her road manager, had to go with her.

But I was plain embarrassed! I mean I was a southern boy from the hills of North Carolina: I'd never been in those kinds of places! So I'm in there and I'm trying not to look around too much. Paulette buys all her stuff, and we leave the store and she starts talking to me, as by then we'd developed a good relationship.

Paulette said, "Now John, I've been thinking, I need a good utility player. And I said, all innocent: "You do?" and she said, "Yeah you know, someone who can play a couple of different instruments?"

I replied, "Well that's funny Paulette, I do know somebody like that!" And she goes "Really?" and I said, "Yeah!" She asked, "Well, who is it?" I replied, "Well it's me." And (remember what I said about one of the risks of being a tech) she was actually surprised, and she asked, "You play?? And I said, "Yes I do." And she said, "Well, OK, we'll talk about that some more."

Now I know that conversation sounds like it could have come right out of that movie *My Cousin Vinnie*, but as it happened we never did talk about it again. What *did* happen was that I told the electric guitar player in the group about it, and he said, "John, I think you ought to learn all the parts, and show up one day on stage, and just shock her."

I said, "OK I'll do it." Paulette had been playing mostly the acoustic parts, except for the lead acoustic part, because the lead guy would play that. So I learned all those parts, until one day we were up in New York, performing with Ronnie Millsap and Kenny Rogers. The first gig where I'd thought I might do it was at an outdoor amphitheater and I was about to go on, and the guitar player was really trying to get me to do it, but I chickened out and I said, "No man, I'm not ready." And he said, "No I think you are!" But I said: "But I don't think I am." I could tell he was disappointed, but no matter what, I wasn't going to mess up the music. That was always sacred to me.

So I waited, and the next gig was in the round. When you play in the round, the supporting band musicians are down in the circle, where the audience can't really see you, and I felt more comfortable, at least starting out, doing it that way. So I played. When it came time to acknowledge her musicians, Paulette started to announce Rick, she said "And on the acoustic lead guitar is Rick… wait THAT's not Rick! That's John!" And it was so funny, and natural, and then she said, "Now John! That was really good!" I replied, "Well get used to it!" From that day on, I played onstage with a touring band. The prophecy I'd made to my parents had come true.

I now had three jobs with Paulette for her weekend gigs: guitar tech, road manager and guitar player, and yes, I was STILL working at PL Marketing through the week.

After some time, Paulette got a new artist manager, by the name of David Skepner. David used to manage Loretta Lynn, at the time that the movie about her life, *Coal Miner's Daughter*, came out. David was a good manager, very good at his job. I really liked him. He was from Los Angeles originally, but by this time lived in Nashville, and was also managing *Riders in the Sky* at the time. The only problem with David was that he had this facade of LA arrogance, or cockiness, that kind of gave off the vibe that if you were local you were a yokel, and it could rub people the wrong way. But I liked him.

I'll never forget when David wanted to meet me, because I was Paulette's road manager. He said to me (this is what I mean by the superior bit): "John listen, I want you to know something (He was trying to be very much the new sheriff in town), and he told me: "You know, I understand that you are road managing her right now, but I wanted you to know, we'll just see how long that lasts."

I didn't bat an eye, and instead I kind of chuckled and said to him "You mean, sort of like you're the manager now, and how long that might last as well?" And I think he probably may have respected me for saying it, but it sure didn't seem he liked it at that point.

Not long after that, we went on a road trip where I handled a difficult situation between Paulette and the Promoter. I made Paulette look good, and didn't make the promoter look bad, and everyone was in a win-win situation. David called me in his office after that road trip, and he was just gushing, like a totally different person. This time he said: "I just want you to know, John, I would not have anybody else in the world on the road with Paulette other than you." I said, "Well I appreciate that David, thank you."

The irony was, even though I was being a Smart Alec at our first meeting, the jury really WAS still out on him, as far as we were concerned. This was because we had not seen any action yet. David had gotten a couple of gigs, but they were lowball gigs in that they paid less than others we had taken. At that point, this was right on the borderline of making money, but not much more than breaking even.

Besides getting higher paying gigs, and record deals, keeping tabs on expenses was the other aspect of being the manager. In those days, by the time you rented a bus, paid for the fuel and the driver, and then paid the musicians, their per diems, and hotel rooms, it all added up. You had to keep an eye on things to make sure you'd make some money. Sometimes, for the exposure, you would take a gig that didn't make any money on ticket sales, as long as it was in the middle of two gigs that did. You could occasionally afford to do that, because you'd sell some merchandise.

The point was, you never really knew how good or bad you were going to do.

Unfortunately, as time went on, David wasn't able to talk to the record label, to find out if they were going to do a second album for Paulette. I think Paulette's husband Randy was getting frustrated with David. I am honestly not sure how well the two of them got along. So less than six months in, Paulette and Randy decided they wanted to make a change.

They called me for dinner again, and although you might think I should have known better by now, I had no idea that they were going to ask me to be the manager. Sure enough, they said: "We'd like you to consider managing Paulette." This time, though, I was incredulous, and tried to say, in a nice way, "You know, I don't have any experience managing an artist. I mean sure, I have some experience now as a road manager, and I get that it's a relationship, but that's the whole point: I don't have any relationships at all with any of the people that are heads of the record labels."

They said, "Yes, but you have business experience, and we've seen that. We believe that you can make those relationships, and we'd like you to consider it."

I said, "Well, I'm not going to make that decision today. I'm just not going to do that." And I also recall saying: "The thing I don't want to do, is anything to screw up Paulette's career. I know this is a great opportunity for anybody to jump at. But I don't want to take it just because it's an opportunity for me. I'm a musician Number 1. That's why I'm here in Nashville." So I went home and I thought about it for about a week or so. Then I called her back, and said, "Well, I guess I'll give this a shot. But anytime I feel like I'm screwing up your career, I'm going to call it quits, and you're going have to find another manager."

So we agreed to that, and that's where the managing role began. A Manager has a different and expanded responsibility than the road manager. An artist manager is in charge of every aspect of the recording artist's career. From hiring the studio musicians, dealing with the record label, dealing with publicity, promoters, other managers, all the things that make a career. So it was a step-up in responsibility, and a full-time job in its own right. But now I was not an artist in my own right. I was the business manager for another artist. However, I felt good about managing, and I made great relationships with the booking agents.

I already had pretty good relationships with them as the road manager, because the road manager has to talk with them. I'd gone to meet with them several times before, and I'd given them several little perks, just as you would in any business relationship you were trying to maintain. We just had really good relationships, good rapport. I was easy to work with, didn't ever try to throw my weight around or be a jerk. But I was also assertive on behalf of my client, which they respected.

When it came to contracts, one thing you had to learn to do was to read them with a fine-tooth comb. This was because sometimes one side or the other would insert weird little conditions that could trip you up if you weren't careful. Sometimes people would put these clauses in to make sure the promoter was reading it and paying attention. Other times they were being truly picky. I remember one artist (not Paulette) asking for "only green M&M's in the green (dressing) room"! Paulette was never demanding that way. Our verbiage was typically very straightforward.

I remember having a meeting with the head of Buddy Lee Attractions, one of the bigger booking agencies in town at the time. He said to me: "I think this is a good move for Paulette, because we like you. You're assertive, but you're not an #?*hole."

Forgive the language, but that's how he put it. There are unfortunately a few of those in Nashville, as there are everywhere, but in any event that part of my new role started off great. The booking side was wonderful, and I got us some decent gigs. I was able to get us some fire hall gigs, which were pretty steady work, and made some decent money. We got some exposure and sold some merchandise.

In contrast, on the recording side, things were not so rosy. Paulette had released her first solo album, *Love Goes On*, with Capitol records, but I was having a heck of a time trying to get hold of them. I had gotten to the point where the head of Capitol Nashville, Jimmy Bowen, who had produced *Love Goes On*, was not returning my calls. In any sales/marketing relationship that is never a good sign. This was still pretty early in my tenure, maybe the beginning of 1992, and I was getting concerned, but it was still far too early to panic.

So I said to Wayne Halper, who was the attorney for Capitol Nashville at the time, "Look Wayne, I like you man, I mean I know we've never met in person, but I enjoy talking to you on the phone, but I really need to talk to Jimmy. I just want to know, one way or another, if he's willing to move forward with another project, or not."

Now just before that, Jimmy had given us money to go in the studio with Jerry Crutchfield, who was a famous producer. Jerry had produced some big acts like Tanya Tucker, and he was a really nice man. It was a great experience to go in the studio with Jerry and watch him produce those records, the musicians he chose, and the background vocals. I really enjoyed that.

Jerry produced four sides, and he put a different twist on each one, a different style. He believed if we did that, then someone like Jimmy Bowen would like it. He would either appreciate the fact that we were versatile enough to do it, or maybe he would pick up on one style and say: "OK let's go with this."

Jimmy should have, because it was really great material. And I'm not saying that just because I was involved. It was Paulette and her sound, and then it was Jerry Crutchfield, and the way he tied everything together.

But Jimmy (Bowen) just sat on it. I could never get a response from him. Finally after about six months of calling I had a conversation with Wayne, and said, a little frustrated by now: "Listen Wayne, this is enough. I need a straight answer from Jimmy, one way or another. You tell him that I need an answer tomorrow morning. I don't care what it is, just give me an answer."

So Wayne called me back the next morning, and I could tell he was nervous as a cat, said, "Well, you know John, we're going to let her (Paulette) go."

And I said "OK, thank you." I'm pretty sure that my response was a surprise to him, because I think he was expecting me to get mad, but I had told him the truth. I really wanted to stop spinning my wheels and just get a straight answer one way or another. Then Wayne said that Jimmy was kind enough to give us those four sides that we'd recorded, which he didn't have to do, and that we could shop them around town if we wanted.

So I did. I shopped it everywhere. Most people were kind, I must say. I remember talking to the guy that produced several well-known artists, who was this really nice fellow from Georgia. I talked with him for an hour in his office. Now just to give you an idea, it was not much of an office, more like a couch and some windows. It was kind of weird, but he was a very nice guy, and he said, "Well John, I just don't think that we're interested at this point, but I really appreciate you, y'know."

I could just hear Elvis saying: "A Little Less Conversation, a Little More Action!"

Although that was a disappointment, which was fine: that's show biz, as they say, and I was cool with that. So I went to some other labels, and who should be at one of the labels, but my old contact Al Cooley, who had given me such encouragement as a songwriter when I'd first come to town.

It was now a couple of years later and he didn't recognize me. I was also going to see him as Paulette's manager. I was pitching her to him, which is a totally different dynamic than a young aspiring songwriter asking for guidance. I was pretty assertive with him. I wasn't aggressive, but I was assertive. Al told me: "You know John, I just don't think we're interested," I replied, "Well, did you listen to them?" He said, "Well yeah, I did just listen to them."

I said, "Well, don't you think they're good?" Al replied "Well, yeah, but we're not interested." I kept pressing: "Well, you know I'm just going to go down here to your competitors, and there are some folks who are kind of interested in this material (of course, this was just a sales tactic, because I had not gotten any real interest yet). Then Al just said: "John, you don't understand, "We're not f@#*ing interested!"

I was completely taken aback. I really was. I'd been in the business long enough that I'd heard people talk that way, but definitely not the Vice President of a label. I mean, not ever. So I just said, "Well OK, but I'm gonna tell you what. I want you to keep that tape, because one day you are going to hear it again, but it ain't gonna be on your tape deck, it's gonna be on the radio."

I got up, and left, and that was the end of that. I'll always remember Al, not just because he was such a weird guy, but for the two very different conversations I had with him: one very nurturing and supportive, the other hardnosed to the point of hostility. But seeing both sides of the business like that was a great experience.

I should probably shed some light on why I was having such a hard time getting Paulette another record deal, and why David must have done as well. As it happened, Paulette's first album had been released six months before I came on. Paulette had sold tens of thousands of units, which is a lot if you're an Indie label, but not for a major label like Capitol Records. They want to see 100,000 units right off the bat. I hadn't known this when I joined Paulette's team, but the tepid level of sales that the first album had was almost certainly preventing them from taking Paulette on again.

It wasn't her fault, but rather an example of how small the music business is. Paulette's manager, before she was on the label, went to work for Capitol Nashville, while he was still her manager, which was a complete conflict of interests. As her manager he was supposed to look out for her interests, but working for the record company he had to look out for their interests. Therefore, if he'd pushed her, that would have looked bad. He actually had to disavow her, which is why she had to find another manager.

Unfortunately, once you get to that point, you get lost in the shuffle. Paulette had a record deal, but her champion couldn't go to bat for her. Her first single, *I'll Start With You*, did pretty well, and charted at #21. Her second one, *Not With My Heart You Don't*, also charted, but her third one, called *The Chain Just Broke*, did nothing, because there was nobody pushing it. By that I mean there was nobody paying the money to the record promoters to radio because it was just lost in the shuffle.

Because the guy who'd been working for her was now working for the label, he had other responsibilities, and had to look out for himself, so every time she'd visit the label it would be "Hey Paulette, how's it going?" and was friendly, but nobody was actually *doing* anything.

Now, although Paulette was and is a musician and artist first, unlike many creative folks she has a lot of business savvy. Because of her past experience with Warner Bros. and *Highway 101*, she recognized the need for someone other than herself to professionally represent her. Due to that conflict of interest, Paulette essentially had nobody representing her interests at a critical time, so her album got totally lost. It really shouldn't have. She had a great, GREAT musical product, but on the business side of things, that's what happened. When I became the manager, I had to come in, and mop all that up. Or try to.

I didn't know most of the background until I had already agreed to be her manager. Then I got filled in on the situation, and I thought to myself: "Wow, this is really a mess!" As I'd feared from the very beginning, it wasn't as if I had a lot of experience on that side of the business, whether with Paulette, or anybody. Nor did I have the relationships with record-label executives that might have opened more doors.

This is similar to what can happen in book publishing. If you sell a book, and it doesn't do very well, the book might be great, and your next book might really be great, but the publishers (in this case the record labels) aren't going to be very keen about investing in you. Even if they look at you, and even if they love your music, if your prior sales haven't been that good, and they've got someone else who, by comparison, has had a ton of sales, they are going to go with the artist who has sold more. This is because they can show they are backing a horse that, in turn, has already shown he or she can win, not one that may have underperformed because something else, something temporary, happened, (like maybe it pulled a muscle).

The attitude is that they are satisfying proven market demand, which is a safer business strategy for them. The fact that poor sales may not reflect the quality of the underlying work, but rather poor marketing that didn't play to the work's strengths, is not going to trouble them too much. At the end of the day, they are in business to make money, which requires analysis of risk and reward.

If talent was thin on the ground, their attitude might be different. But in the music business, certainly in Nashville, there are many crazy-talented artists flooding into town every day, with great material. There is too much competition for executives to worry about losing out on a product that didn't sell well, whatever the reason. When it comes to the bottom line (which is what they are measured on) their model makes perfect sense to them. So if you or I miss out on hearing an amazing talent as a result, there's a lot of other amazing (or at least popular) talent that they are bringing to market.

Technology has come a long way over the past few years, to help musicians and songwriters become more successful as independently published or self-published artists. You now have places like CD Baby, and platforms like iTunes, Spotify, etc.. who can help get your music out there. This is a double-edged sword, because although you don't have to rely on big record labels as a musician so much anymore it is still ridiculously competitive. There is a LOT more "noise."

Technology has also helped bring the cost of production down. Whereas it used to cost tens of thousands of dollars just to produce an album, now you can record, mix, and master ten tracks in a really good studio in Nashville for much less. Finally, physical copy sales are giving way to streaming sales. Things are changing all the time for the independent artist. It's still by no means easy, but at least your work stays yours.

However, back in the early 90's you were still pretty much at the mercy of the record labels to try and get an album produced. So with Paulette's first album, even though the songs were really good, the album didn't sell well, and so it was an uphill battle trying to find a label for a new one.

This is where my prior marketing experience became relevant. When I couldn't get anyone to release a second album, and I couldn't get anyone else to sign Paulette, we decided we'd do a Christmas album. We did this on her independent label. I knew Paulette had enough name recognition to get some sales, and I knew it would be repeating sales, even if seasonal, for probably a few years into the future.

The name of the album was *Christmas is for You*. Paulette had written two songs on the album, the first of which was called *Mrs. Santa Claus*, (which was the name of the video.) The second was the eponymous track: *Christmas is for You*, which goes "This year Jesus, Christmas is for you."

Right about now, if you were thinking that I had done a lot within Paulette's organization in a pretty short period of time, you would be right. I'd started as a lowly guitar tech in 1991. By the end of 1992, I'd become a road manager and utility player. Now I was a Manager! If that sounds like a meteoric rise in an organization, in one way it was. But I was keenly aware I didn't have any direct experience with the music business itself. A lot of the skill set I had acquired working in the food industry was transferable. But I was feeling very stressed, as I really wanted to do a good job for Paulette, and didn't have a lot of "street cred" in Nashville.

Despite that, we started recording the Christmas album in August/September of 1992, and released it in October of that same year. But we had no distribution channel as yet. That became my next job. I knocked on a lot of doors, but couldn't get any interest. Then, whether it was a burst of creativity, or desperation, or both, I approached Kroger's, because of my relationships there, to get them to place orders.

Nowadays you can walk into Kroger's and in almost every store see DVD's for sale, but I don't think Kroger's had done anything like that yet, to the best of my knowledge: So we got the CDs and Cassettes in Kroger's, (which was the only place I could get a commitment at first). Then we were also very fortunate to get the record in Ingram distribution. Ingram was a big distributor in town. I had a meeting with those guys in this large boardroom (like a conference room you see on TV). This was the first time I'd been in a space or a meeting like that, and I was in charge.

I vividly remember being asked, "Well, how many units do you think it (the album) is going to sell?" Wouldn't you know, that's the one thing I hadn't really thought about! Before I could say anything, because I was really about to freeze, Paulette's husband Randy, who was sitting right next to me, says: "Oh we fully expect this to sell 50,000 units the first year."

I nudged him, to say, "Thanks, I appreciate that!" The Ingram folks were nodding to each other, as if to say, "Well that's a pretty good number." And it was a smart number to put out there: big enough to let them think it was worth their while, but not so big to make them think we'd lost touch with reality. But inside I was thinking: "There is no way we're going to sell 50,000 units, especially with such a short amount of time until Christmas."

Of course, we did NOT sell 50,000 units; we were lucky if we sold a thousand that first Christmas. This is where the rubber met the road, so to speak, on the business side of things, and with my stress level. I owed $100,000 to the company who'd duplicated the album, so I had to hold him off for a whole year until I could sell it again. By the summer of 1993 we were hemorrhaging money. We had paid to record the album and duplicate it, and now we had to produce the video.

When we shot the video, I was also the one who needed to deal with the producer to ensure that things went smoothly on that front as well. This was a whole other experience set that I learned on the fly. We shot that video with 16 mm film, and organized that shoot in LA somewhere in a canyon in the suburbs. We had all those little people there (I learned pretty quickly they liked to be called little people, not midgets). We did the shoot for well under the going price for music videos.

The most expensive part of that production was the little people. Without getting too specific, let's just say they were very excited to be around a whole lot of other people who looked like them, and they got up to all kinds of shenanigans. (If you've heard stories about the munchkins during the filming of *The Wizard of Oz*, I'd be willing to bet they were all true). I couldn't do too much, because of their value to the show, of which they were fully aware, let me tell you.

But we did finally finish the shoot for *Mrs. Santa Claus*, and got the film "in the can" as they used to say.

Meanwhile, I was having very difficult conversations with the people to whom we owed money, most notably the individual who had duplicated the album. These conversations were very stressful as well. They went a lot like the ones between a deadbeat tenant and a landlord who wants his rent. He kept asking, "Where's my money?" I kept telling him: "You know this is a Christmas album, I'm going to get you your money, but it will have to be next Christmas!" He would say, "Yeah I hear that all the time man." He was hammering me. It was one of the worst times, in terms of stress, that I had ever experienced.

On the other hand, I did make some good relationships during the rest of that year, and got a great distribution deal with another company. The next Christmas (1993), we sold 30,000 units. We were finally out of debt and made a profit. So it could be done, even with the way things were then, but if I'd had the Internet and Facebook back then, I really believe we would have cracked 100,000 units.

But we had to wait all the way through 1993 for this to happen.

Meanwhile, as if all of this wasn't enough, during this time I met and married my second wife, Mary, the woman who would become the mother of my children. Mary and I met when I was playing on the road with Paulette. We were playing in Minnesota, in an Indian casino on the reservation in 1992 when we met, and Mary later moved down to Nashville. We got married in 1993, the same year I had the guy from the CD-copying company hammering me for his hundred grand.

Mary had a son from her first marriage, named Tyler, and I adopted him. Later on, my daughter Makenzy was born in November 1996, followed by Reagan in October 2000.

As I was settling in with my new marriage, the Christmas album sold enough copies to get us out of debt, but then began another journey of struggle and anxiety. One day, the summer after we released the Christmas album, Randy and I were riding together to meet Paulette at the house of some friends of theirs. As we were talking, he said to me, "Well, you know John, I'm thinking about taking her (Paulette) back up to Alaska for a while."

You could have knocked me over with a feather! When I finally managed to ask why, he said they needed a break. In retrospect,

I can see why they might have thought so. At the time I had gone through the strain of recording the Christmas album in record time, followed by a hastily put together Christmas tour, dealing for months with an irate creditor, and putting together a music video. Heck, I needed a break too.

I reminded Randy about the money we owed the duplicator, but Randy didn't seem too worried about that. "It will get paid," he said, and I knew myself getting an entire year to plan the marketing for the next Christmas, sales would be significantly better. But I felt that something wasn't right and finally he said: "Look, you're going to be fine. When we're gone, when she's gone, you're gonna have a job at a record label, or managing somebody else, you're going to be fine." At that point I was kind of dumbfounded, because I wasn't thinking about my position, but Paulette's career.

I wasn't thinking about "I'm going to lose my position," it was more like "We've put so much work into promoting her, and developing her brand."

Randy and Paulette had set up a business called Sportsman Music Inc., and Paulette's business, Paulette Carlson Entertainment, was the management side of it. I was the manager. We were actively seeking new artists to manage as well.

Fortunately, 1993 proved to be a successful one for the Christmas album. I secured a better distribution deal and more effective marketing, which resulted in significant sales and allowed us to pay all the creditors and investors, with a little left over.

Now we needed to build on that success, so one day after much thought, I said to Paulette, "Look here's what I think needs to

happen. We need to have a reunion tour with *Highway 101*."
Paulette had left *Highway 101* in 1988, two years before the
Love Goes On album came out in 1990, at the height of their
popularity. As far as I could tell, one or two of the other band
members didn't like the fact that Paulette had expressed an
interest in developing an acting career, alongside her music
career with them. I never really understood that, because if she'd
successfully broken into acting, her increased visibility would
surely have helped drive album sales and concert tickets (as I
knew full well: remember Elvis!)

Anyhow, the bass player from *Highway 101* was a really good guy
named Curtis Stone. I knew Curtis' Dad, Cliffie Stone, who was a
country singer, musician, record producer, music publisher, and
radio and TV personality. One day, Cliffie and I ended up out in
LA playing at the same concert. While we were backstage, we got a
chance to talk privately. It was funny because I'd already thought
that the best thing for Paulette might be for the band to get back
together. So in this conversation Cliffie was soft-pedaling me on
the same idea, and I was soft-pedaling him, when he just looked
at me and said: "Well do you think this could happen?"

I said that I could make sure that Paulette would be in, if he
could make it happen with the rest of them. Cliffie replied,
"Well I can make it happen with my son (Curtis, the bass
player), and probably with Jack (Daniels, the guitarist, unrelated
to the whiskey company!), but I don't know about the drummer
(Scott "Cactus" Moser)."

I said, "Well that's OK, let's go to work on it!" So we started
that dialogue, and we talked back and forth on the phone, etc.
We finally got everyone to agree except the drummer, Cactus
Moser. I talked to Jim Ed Norman a couple of times at Warner
Bros. I told him, "I've got them all together except the drummer."

He said, "Well that's not good enough, but if you get the drummer, you've got the deal."

Now, given all the jokes about drummers, you might find it odd that nobody would want to record the band without this one drummer. But you have to understand that the drummer is often a critical part of a band's sound. Lots of otherwise decent bands have fallen by the wayside due to subpar drumming, and a great drummer can make an otherwise mediocre band sound better than they really are. Plus, if you have a drummer who intimately knows a band's sound and feel, he can get the other musicians to groove together way better than somebody who doesn't feel the music.

Also, the record label's marketing department had already seen the lackluster sales performance of a "partial *Highway 101*," (without Paulette), so, all the jokes aside, anything less than all four original members would not work in their minds. They were thinking that *Highway 101* wouldn't be *Highway 101* without everyone, including its original drummer.

But I was unable to do it! Cactus and I definitely didn't' see eye to eye, for some reason. Jack, Curtis and Cliffie all worked on him as well, but to no avail. He was not going to have any part of it.

Trying to piece it together, I suspect Cactus' feelings got hurt when Paulette left. One day, a few years afterwards, I ran into Curtis Stone (the bassist) in a Home Depot, of all places. Now I really liked Curtis, he was a very down to earth person. While we were talking, he said, "Well you know what happened don't you?" I said, "Well no, not really, I'd really like to know. What did happen, I mean you guys had it made man, you were just about to hit the STRIDE, you know, take that next big step?"

Curtis said: "It was because she wanted to go and act, and we didn't want her to."

And I said, "Well why in the world not? That doesn't make any sense to me. I mean here you had this woman who could have brought you even more exposure!"

Curtis replied: "I totally agree with you now John, it's like looking back always gives you 20/20 vision. We should have let her do what she wanted to do, and we could have stayed together as a group. But at the time, we just couldn't see it that way."

So I asked: "Well why didn't you get together again when you had the opportunity to do it?" And he said, "Well because the drummer wouldn't do it." Which we all knew, but the big question was: Why not?

I never really got a straight answer to that question, and it was just too bad, but it happens quite a lot: You have people who are getting famous, and approaching, if not quite the top of the world, at least to the place where they can see the peak, and the differences that occur start to take their toll. If there's one thing I am sure of, it's this: Any group of musicians who are calling themselves a band or duo or trio or a name of any kind and are recording together, should always create a legal contract spelling out in detail the specifics, so as to protect the entity and its assets.

At the time I was trying to get them all back together, Cactus and I really didn't get on well together. I knew they'd have NO shot at a reunion if I stayed in the picture. So it seemed to me that the best thing I could do for Paulette at this point, then, was to step aside. So in 1995 I told Paulette, "You know, at this point Paulette, I believe it's best for you that I leave."

Chapter 5

SLAP-DOWN
Life in the Fast Lane

With Paulette I'd gone from guitar tech to road manager to guitar player to artist manager in a span of only a few years. I'd also remarried, so there was a lot going on, with the kind of stress that a lot of change in a relatively short time span can bring you. I was busy, and I was becoming increasingly "successful" by some benchmarks. But I also wasn't playing as much music as I had imagined I would be when I first came to town. I wasn't writing any of my own material. I sure wasn't developing my own career as a musician, but trying to develop the careers of others. I wasn't charting my own course, but rather navigating somebody else's ship.

If God was trying to speak to me during this time, I don't think I could even be accused of ignoring His voice. Rather, there was so much "noise" I was probably deaf to it. I could tear myself in pieces trying to figure whether I was heedless of God's call, but even when we choose not to listen (or have become deaf) we are still here for God's purpose, and he still finds a way to realize that purpose in our lives.

Today, living in the most integrated way I have ever been, I sometimes think: If I'd known THIS at THAT TIME, I might have made different choices. On the other hand, maybe I had to make those choices so I could learn what I needed to learn, in such a way that I would never forget it, so that maybe, just maybe, I could become the person that God wanted me to be. So it could be that the decisions that seemed to lead me to follow my will, and not God's, were instead the preparation to become the person I am today. Or both. What I might characterize or label as "mistakes" may not necessarily have been mistakes, they just might have been necessary.

In any event, when I told Paulette I needed to leave, she understood my reasoning, and we parted as friends. By this time, I had also begun to work with three other performers besides Paulette. One group in particular that approached me, The McCarters had released albums on Warner Bros. Records, but currently did not have a record deal.

Although my career as a musician hadn't evolved as I had thought it would, this was largely through my own choices. Despite leaving Paulette, I was increasingly busy on the professional side. My career had all the trappings of an upward trajectory. I had an office on Music Row; I had been involved with several professional acts. Now I was looking to take that next step.

On the personal dimension, though, things were not so good. The stresses in my personal life, combined with the stress in my professional life, began to take a toll on my health.

I'd met my second wife, Mary in 1992, when I was playing guitar with Paulette at a casino in Minnesota, Mary's home state. I remember meeting her, and flirting with her and then I didn't hear from her again. I came back home to Nashville, and was on a spring tour that started in Texas then through Arizona, New Mexico, on to California, and through Montana (where we rode through a pretty good Spring snowstorm in the Mountains). One day, after getting home, I got a phone call from Mary right out of the blue and at first I didn't even remember her! So she had to refresh my memory about that until finally, it dawned on me who she was. I invited her down for Easter, and she came down for a visit.

I was taken in by Mary's charm at the time and we were married in 1993. I could write so much about my marriage to Mary, and its struggles, but that's not as important as the sum of the marriage, which are my three children: Tyler, whom I adopted, Makenzy, and Reagan. I'm so thankful that God allowed me to be their father. Though I could say many more positive things about my children, it's kind of like pulling your wallet out to show photos at a party, I would be way more interested than you!

Although there are many details I could share about my personal life, and about the fault lines in my marriage, this book, again, is not intended as a "tell-all," but I will say this: I suppose that, even though I was on the business side of the music industry, conducting hard-nosed negotiations, I still have that softer musician aspect to my personality. I tend to think the best of people, and when life is stressful, and you are pretty confident in most areas, but are feeling insecure about how competent you are on one or two other dimensions, certain kinds of people can tell. They capitalize on it. They tell you how great you are, and make you feel good about yourself, until they have their hooks into you, and they start humming a different tune. It takes a long time and a lot of energy to break out of that kind of dynamic.

Without going into specifics, I believe that Mary was one of those people. And I cannot discount the mixed messages that I was experiencing in my marriage as a contributing factor to my overall stress level.

One silver lining was the fact that my parents moved to Nashville around the time I met and married Mary. They ended up buying 60 acres of which they gave me 5 to build a house next to the one they built. My folks aren't demonstrative with their feelings, but we've always had a very solid and loving relationship, as you'd expect in a family with an only child, and this was a typical example of how they showed their love. I'd been in Nashville for about five years by this time, and I guess they figured I was going to stay, so they decided to move to Nashville in order to be closer. They have a pretty calm approach to things. I suspect their presence helped me deal with a lot of the turmoil in my life. I was very thankful to have them near, especially after my stroke.

After my parents' move to the Nashville area, I made another business decision that would have a profound effect on my life. My dad and I bought a carpet cleaning franchise through a company called Chem-Dry. When you get to a certain point in the industry, you come to realize that the money you are making won't last forever, especially if you are not making residual income from things like music or merchandise sales. As a manager, you can negotiate those things eventually, but I was still not at a point where the acts I was representing were doing a lot of that. It made sense to me to have something to which could provide an income stream when I was no longer in the music business.

The combined stresses and uncertainties of my personal and professional lives were beginning to take their toll.

I developed high blood pressure, for which I needed to start taking medication. If you were self-employed as I was, you pretty much had to pay for your own health care out-of-pocket. When I'd been with PL Marketing, I'd had health insurance through my employer. Since I'd left them to manage Paulette I didn't have that benefit. But I was still a relatively young man, and healthy. Private health insurance was expensive, so I didn't have health insurance. As a result, when I developed high blood pressure, I didn't really get the best health care or guidance. I had different doctors at different times, so an important thing in the medical field, called "continuity of care," was missing. This basically meant that if I saw a new doctor, he or she would not know what a previous doctor had diagnosed, or prescribed, for me. The new doctor could therefore prescribe a new medication that might or might not be appropriate.

The last tour I arranged, before God allowed my devastating wake up call, was with Jennifer McCarter of The McCarters. Unfortunately, even this ended up being a nightmare, because her sisters didn't come! The McCarters were Jennifer, who was the eldest, and the twins Lisa and Teresa, who were a couple of years younger. Like megastar Dolly Parton, The McCarters were from Sevierville, Tennessee, and Ms. Parton had in fact had them on her Dolly variety show.

By the time I met them, the act was called *Jennifer McCarter and The McCarters*. They'd had some good success in the late 1980's, with their first album, *The Gift*, charting at #36 on the U.S. Country charts (and the single of the same name charting at #4). It was in support of *The Gift* that Ms. Parton had them on her show, and this exposure, combined with the worldwide tour they did with Randy Travis (whose manager, Kyle Lehning, also repped the sisters) is likely what helped that debut album to chart so well.

Their second album *Better Be Home Soon*, didn't chart, even though a single from that album, *Up and Gone*, was a top-10 hit in the U.S. and Canada. In keeping with the "What have you done for me lately?" reality of the record labels, Warner Bros. dropped The McCarters in 1990 after the relatively disappointing performance of *Better Be Home Soon*.

Better Be Home Soon focused more on Jennifer's vocal talents, and less on the harmonies that had been a hallmark of their earlier success, which may have been a factor in its lukewarm reception. By 1995, when they approached me to manage them, The McCarters had spent roughly five years focusing on live shows, celebrity appearances, and endorsements, and were looking to make a musical comeback. I thought the material they were developing sounded really promising, especially as there was more of the harmonizing that had made their first album so successful.

There were some relationships in Europe that needed to be repaired, due to some miscommunication before I had taken over, in order for them to tour over there again. I was able to develop a good working relationship with promoters from Switzerland and the Netherlands, so we were able to do a tour in the summer. It was during this tour that I further strengthened our position for return tours. I also developed a timeline for foreign investment for a Christmas album, for which The McCarters would tour at Christmas of 1996.

The investment contract called for one album, which would be a Christmas album. When asking for the investment money, I asked for enough to record two albums worth of music unbeknownst to the investor. My intention was to provide a bonus for his investment. By touring at Christmas with a new Christmas album, this would help "pre-launch" the bonus

Country album by reintroducing the act to a foreign audience, one that had always liked their music. Then, once the album was ready, there'd already be a "buzz" about the group, and a summer tour in support of the new album would have a higher chance of success.

Unfortunately, (remember God and his sense of humor?) things didn't go according to plan. Not long before the European tour was supposed to start, Lisa and Teresa came to me stating they flatly refused to go on tour with Jennifer! It really isn't my place to disclose why the twins made this decision. All I will say is they were righteously angry, and felt justified. In any event, I couldn't talk them out of it.

The result of this family conflict changed the whole dynamic of the tour! I had to scramble to find new musicians, especially backup vocals to Jennifer. Sadly, Jennifer didn't have the star power to overcome the loss of her sisters to the tour. As a result, the tour struggled financially. On the personal side, I was missing my daughter, Mackenzy, who had been born November 1, 1996. I was also dealing with feelings of anxiety resulting from the way the dynamics with Mary had me feeling continuously off-balance.

I started to experience some adverse side effects from the blood pressure medicine I was on, and my blood pressure wasn't being well controlled anyway. I was also getting occasional chest pain. So when I got back to Nashville I went to see my doctor of the moment, to see what could be done.

Nothing particularly worked, and then one day early in 1997, one doctor gave me a sample of a blood pressure drug called Cardizem-SR, telling me to take it at bedtime. Cardizem-SR is a slow release, long-acting form of a class of drugs known as calcium channel blockers. This drug class is effective for high blood pressure, as well as for helping people with angina (chest pain due to a lack of blood going through the arteries in the heart).

I took the drug at bedtime, as prescribed, and went to sleep. It took me 20 years to learn why being given this drug, especially in its slow release (SR) form, especially taken at bedtime, was likely not the best medical advice I could have received, given my medical history.

When I woke up the next morning, my life had changed forever!

Chapter 6

STROKED BY GOD
Foggy Mental Breakdown

The word "stroke," like the word "cancer," is a generic word used to explain a variety of states, which may be very different in presentation and cause. Generally speaking, when blood flow to the brain, or a particular area of the brain, is cut off, that part of the brain is deprived of oxygen. If that state persists for too long, brain damage begins to occur.

Such damage is permanent, so in VERY basic terms, your ability to recover from a "stroke" depends on how well other, undamaged parts of your brain can get "rewired," to pick up the slack. Sometimes, the damage is too extensive for this to happen. Sometimes it isn't, but the length of time it takes to recover anything at all varies greatly from one person to the next.

Did I have a stroke? I don't really know. The best medical answer is "most likely not." I say this because stroke symptoms usually have a deficit on one side of their body, or brain. But my physical abilities were never hampered. I did, however have a global reduction in my ability to reason, speak and generally interact with people.

I didn't have medical insurance, so I didn't seek medical care in a timely way after my event. Without the necessary tests (which I never received), it is difficult to pinpoint exactly how and where the blood flow to my noggin was compromised. But it seems clear that for some period of time my brain didn't get enough oxygen, and I lost a great deal of my cognitive abilities.

It seems possible that the slow release Cardizem was mostly responsible. But even that explanation remains, at best, informed speculation put together after many years, and without me having had a physical evaluation or diagnosis following the event. The prescribing physician was certainly in no rush to discover whether a medication he had placed me on might be responsible for what happened to me.

Exactly how my brain was damaged, and how it has managed to heal, remain questions to which I can never receive a definite answer in this lifetime. Damaged I certainly was. My healing, though miraculous, was difficult and slow.

Upon waking up the morning after I took the Cardizem-SR, the thing I most recall is that my eyes were squeezed and crusted so tightly shut that I could not open them. Everything on my body was swollen beyond belief. I felt as if I looked like the Michelin Man! A lot of the rest is a blank, or so fuzzy and incoherent as to be pretty useless for the purposes of telling a story. Setting my memories down on paper has proved to be a healing exercise. Many memories that were lost to me for years have returned. Many events that were jumbled up in my brain are now in their proper sequence. But when I first began writing this book, I couldn't even recall the year I'd had my stroke!

I know it sounds crazy not to remember the date of such a pivotal moment in your life, but that is what a stroke does, or can do, to your memories. They can become jumbled. It's only by comparing things against events that you know to have happened, and have a clear date for, that you can piece together, like Sherlock Holmes digging around in your head by a process of elimination, when certain other events must have happened.

I still find it amazing that I cannot directly orient myself in time to some of those watershed moments. Even now, 20 years later, full memory has not returned. So I turned to my parents to see if they could shed light on things I'd forgotten. My folks had been living in Nashville for about five years around the time that I had my stroke. It was obviously pretty tough on them to see me like that. They are both still alive, and I have asked them about what I was like as well as what it was like for them, given my own lack of clear memories of that time.

When I asked mom and dad to give their perspective on those experiences, they didn't really have much to say. Although we are a very tight knit family we don't talk a whole bunch about our feelings. My Mom, Dad and I maintain a privacy around our feelings for each other, sometimes even with each other.

They did share, with a certain amount of humor after the distance of 20 years (though it wasn't funny at the time), about how big my head got [literally and not because I thought a lot of myself], and for how long it stayed that way after the event. It was very traumatic for them to witness this sudden change that came out of nowhere. But that is the thing they most clearly remember, and of course they were very concerned whether I would recover, and come back as I was before.

They worried deeply about what had happened to me. Nobody really seemed sure how to explain it. Not having health insurance, I lacked access to any ongoing professional help with rehabilitation. This might be why my journey back from my stroke took as long as it did, but it also may be what was necessary for my healing and that the time it took was the time it took.

However, I do remember waking up that first day and my eyes being swollen shut, because it was such a shock to me. I also remember my head being huge and the classic symptoms of a droopy left eye and drooling. For a long time afterwards: it seemed as if a large part of who I was fell asleep, or went into hibernation. Certainly, I became lost to myself for a time.

Even long afterwards (and I'm talking several years), I remained pretty numb. I didn't really think about much, and I'm not even sure if I could think very well. I certainly couldn't continue as anybody's personal artist manager: I simply didn't have the mental faculties anymore. I remember one day the promoter from Europe called, wanting an update on the status of the album, and my wife at the time, Mary, basically telling him about my event. He insisted on speaking to me, and she ultimately let him talk to me for a few minutes, but I could hardly string together a sentence. He got the picture that I was reduced to a shadow of my former self. The stroke was the most dramatic message I could have received that I was not meant to be a music manager anymore. More importantly, it pinpointed the time when I began to give more to God with whatever I had left.

The worst thing of all was that I couldn't play anything anymore. My musical gift, which, with my determination and training, and long hours of practicing and playing on the road, had simply vanished overnight. My muscle memory (which is what takes over in musicians and athletes when you train to a point that you don't need to think about what you are doing, you just do it) had completely gone. I remember picking up a guitar for the first time, and kind of looking at it, trying to just remember how to hold it properly. I'd lived my dream of playing my guitar in front of 50,000 fans at a time, and I couldn't play a single chord.

It's a heck of a thing to wake up one day and discover that, literally overnight, nearly every bit of knowledge that you needed to function in the world has been taken away from you. I had this incredible mental fog, a mist through which I could now barely make sense of the world around me.

I was so numb, both mentally and emotionally, that the fact that I'd lost my abilities, both in business, and as a musician, did not cause me the emotional trauma that you might expect. I've come to believe maybe that is how God protected me at the time, and perhaps moving forward from that time. I sense that being acutely aware of what was happening then may have been too much for me at an emotional or spiritual level. Being somewhat insulated from the memory of events, and as a result not having my emotions so tightly bound up with the implications of those events, might have let me not be overwhelmed by them.

But I didn't forget everything, even at the time, and I didn't forget everything forever. One of the first events that struck an emotional chord was my dad taking me on a car ride one day. This would have been a few months after the stroke, in the early spring of 1997. Dad wanted to get a part for his tractor, so he took me with him. I had not been out of the house for a long time other than to go to the doctor. Dad took me for a long ride somewhere, maybe near Lewisburg (which is south of Nashville, whereas Springfield is north). I remember him having a conversation with me and me just barely being able to keep up my end, and he could tell.

I vividly recall the expression on my father's face. I understood at the time that the hurt look in his eyes had to do with the condition I was in. To this day I remember that look and thinking at the time: "Gosh I don't want him to see me this way, and I don't want to see myself this way either."

When you have a stroke, or are recovering from stroke-like events, you are very aware of the impact your condition has on other people. This is especially true of those who are or have been close to you, and can remember how you used to be before the event. There is a weird combination of emotions that happens as a result: you don't want people you care about to feel that pain. You don't want people who knew what you were like before to see the way you are now and make that comparison. There's a strong sense of trying to protect people, while simultaneously feeling self-conscious and ashamed. You don't want them feeling sorry for you while you are fighting so hard to come back, which never happens as quickly as you want it to, so together with all the other emotions you feel frustrated and angry as well.

All of the above was certainly true for me. I felt angry, self-conscious, and ashamed. I didn't want people in my "old life" (the music business) to know what had happened to me. I didn't want them to "see me like this." Again, in the "what have you done for me lately" mindset of the music business, especially as I wasn't making an effort to stay on people's minds, I sank out of sight in the Nashville music business almost as quickly as I lost my ability to play the guitar. I was a "might-have-been" who didn't even get the chance to be a "has-been." This was probably O.K., as I'm not sure how I would have responded if people had made a big fuss.

Remember that carpet cleaning business I'd bought as a side investment? It became my livelihood. I couldn't book a concert tour to save my life, nor could I play any instrument. However, despite the mental fog I operated in for several years, I was still a relatively young man and had always been physically strong. I could do physical labor. My dad helped me get around and work my carpet cleaning business, until I could figure out how to operate on that level by myself.

One episode that brought home this juxtaposition of physical aptitude and mental fog was one day when I was trying to put together a metal swing set for Tyler. I recall standing outside looking at the instructions, for what seemed like hours, trying to figure it all out, to no avail, when my next-door neighbor came over and very kindly asked me if he could help. I said yes. We put the swing set together, and I appreciated his help more than he could ever know.

I knew I wanted my music back; that was the first strong desire I remember feeling, once I could feel again. So eventually I pulled my guitar out and tried to play. It was very frustrating for a while. I remember sitting in my bedroom trying to remember things, trying to remember anything! But at first, I just couldn't do it.

I'd literally break out in a cold sweat, trying so hard to mentally force my fingers into the correct positions on the frets, positions where they had once flown so effortlessly, and which now it took so much work to find. Sometimes I'd shed tears of anger, or frustration, or grief, for the lost ability that I could now barely remember. It was worse than being a little kid again, looking at that blue sheet that came with my first guitar, trying to teach myself to play before I could take lessons.

I had every reason in the world to give up, but for whatever reason I just… didn't. And as time went on I'd begin to have what I came to call these little awakenings. Six months passed, and I was able to remember how to play something. I began to notice that in roughly six-month intervals I'd remember a little bit more, then a little bit more. One day I just KNEW God was going to bring it all back to me eventually. I also knew that when He did so, my music would then be entirely for Him. Which is maybe what He'd wanted all those days ago on the Tar River, when I was too busy to listen, or too deaf to hear, or maybe even too busy trying to be cool.

I felt my mental fog as an almost tangible thing, but, like most fogs, I felt it would one day be burned away. That wasn't a feeling I could put into words at the time, you understand, it was just where I was in my heart vs. where I was in my brain. My little awakenings weren't just musical, either. One day, after I'd been operating the carpet cleaning equipment to make a living, probably the spring of 1998, I was walking down the street, trying to clear my head, when suddenly, I heard birds chirping and noisy insects for the first time in over a year.

Now I'm pretty sure that they'd been chirping the whole time, but this time I NOTICED. I was so overwhelmed by the simple pleasure that hearing these birds and insects brought me. I was moved nearly to tears. Another awakening of this kind involved the feel of a breeze blowing against my face, which I interpreted as a reassurance from God. All of these little miracles, which I'd taken for granted in my helter-skelter life of a Nashville music manager, trying to take his career to the next level, suddenly became really meaningful and valuable.

I was having my little musical re-awakenings, and also re-experiencing the joy of the small miracles of God's creation, and doing both as a child would: with wonder when they happened, and with trust looking forward to the next one. And the way that God healed my brain was unmistakably the way musicians learn how to play a song: take a little bit at a time, and repeat it, and repeat it, and repeat it again, until it becomes a part of your long term memory, and the muscles that you use to evoke the tune can almost get there on their own, with very little input from you at a conscious level.

I began learning music again like the child I had been and sensing creation again the way a child might. I think this was because in several important ways I had become as a child. This is when I began to understand that what had happened to me was a blessing, and not the curse so many would think it to be, including myself. For who among adults has not wished to experience again those joyous moments that usually only happen when we are children? And how many of us actually get to do that?

So I started playing what I could remember over and over again, until I had it, and then, like clockwork, God would give me a little more. I would work on it the same way, until I could play an entire song! Wow! I felt like one of those birds being hand-fed by a gentle master. That was the moment when I truly began to understand, at a deep level in my body and not as an abstraction in my brain, what the word redemption meant.

God had granted me the wonderful gift of music, allowed me to use it for my own satisfaction, and then, through a series of my own choices, whereby I placed myself in a position of ill health, allowed me to lose it. But He did not take His hand from me, and He allowed me to gain it back, though that road was difficult and seemed to take forever. The words "are we there yet?" never seem more apt as when you are on a road trip with God.

The journey back to wholeness started very slowly at first. Months passed between awakenings. My mental fog only melted away gradually, over the course of years. While the fog cleared, I cleaned carpets, and bit-by-bit the music came back to me.

Then one day, after recovering sufficiently from a mental standpoint, God stepped in again. Despite feeling so closely connected to God once again, I don't remember going to church a lot after the stroke. I was raised Presbyterian, remember, but Mary was Lutheran and after we got married she and I decided to go to the Methodist Church, which was a reasonable compromise. It's a good way to "split the middle," so to speak. So we went there for a while, though I didn't like it much. Then the stroke happened, and I got out of the habit of going to church at all.

In other words, formal worship wasn't something I was doing a lot. However, after several years, it came about that we wanted more of a challenge for our oldest, Tyler, than the public school in Springfield that he attended offered him.

We decided to check out a school called White House Christian Academy, which was in the town of White House, Tennessee, just east of Springfield, where I live. This school was a Church of Christ affiliated school. We liked the people and thought, "Well this'll be good for him," so we placed him there.

My marriage to Mary was troubled, and ended in very painful circumstances. But even though someone causes you a lot of pain, they can still serve a purpose God has for you that will bring you good. We liked the school, but were concerned about the school fees. While we were speaking with the principal afterwards, without asking me, Mary suddenly spoke up and said: "You know John has his music degree and is a professional musician. As you all don't have a music program perhaps we could get a break on the fees if he developed that for you."

I thought to myself: "I don't want to do that!" I couldn't believe she offered that up. But the principal said, "O.K., I would consider that in exchange for his (Tyler's) tuition". But I was still pretty foggy mentally from the stroke, still feeling very self-conscious, and I didn't want to do it. Of course, this was all just my ego talking and operating from a place of fear. I certainly wasn't involving God in the conversation at that point. He was now done with giving me gentle hints. As a reminder to me of how far he had brought me, he allowed me to have a heart attack.

As I was still a young and healthy specimen, the medical explanation for this heart attack is, once again, most likely due to the medication I was on at the time. I had yet to be given a good explanation for what had happened to me in 1997, but after my stroke I had been placed on an older medication. I only discovered later that, if taken for a long period of time, this subsequent medicine could cause a heart attack, which it possibly did. Again, there was no way to know for sure.

While on this medication, I clearly remember falling asleep, while standing up operating a carpet cleaning buffer machine! To this day, I am very leery of taking any kind of medication or supplement. After this, however, I was finally able to see a cardiologist, who knew what he was talking about, and who gave me some decent medical advice. He told me that 80% of my heart was in good shape, and that I should also live to see the age of 80. I remember the two 80's very well. Out of nowhere, my inner negotiator reared his little head, and I said: "Well, that's not good enough, I was hoping for 90!"

It was this cardiologist who first suggested that my event in 1997 might have been a stroke, even though not all the symptoms were consistent with a stroke.

After my heart attack, I decided it might be time to finally smarten up and pay attention to God's will and not my own. So I started teaching music. This is one of the huge ironies in my story, because in order to graduate with my music degree I had promised my professor that I would never try to teach music! The other irony is that a woman who ended up betraying me had a hand in that decision, which did so much to accelerate my healing.

This was how the first place I started attending regular worship again was at a Church of Christ school. Now, for people who may not be familiar with all the possible Christian denominations, especially here in the South, I should explain that the Church of Christ is a fairly strict, scripturally oriented church. I started teaching there, and, perhaps inevitably, we ended up having a difference of opinion on the interpretation of Scripture. This had to do with the place of certain music and the playing of certain music within the school program.

I had been teaching the children to sing a song that a friend of mine, Jim Weatherly (who wrote *Midnight Train to Georgia*) had written, called *Happy Birthday Jesus*, for the Christmas program. The school authorities were upset because by strict interpretation of the Scripture they did not believe that December 25th was Jesus' birthday. They may well be right, of course, but my response was: "Who cares?" My viewpoint was that Jesus' actual birthday could have been July 7, but late December is the time that the world celebrates it, and we were only wishing him Happy Birthday!

I took a stand. I said: "You know, I like this song. I think it's got good meaning for the kids, they've been working hard practicing it, they really like it, and it would be a shame for them not to be able to follow through with it."

Because I pushed back, there was finally a compromise where we finally said, "How we love you Jesus," which in my mind was ridiculous. But I thought, "What the heck, O.K. I'll appease them, I don't want a big fight over this at Christmas." (Which is pretty ironic if you think about it).

It wasn't long after that I left. The writing was on the wall, and I couldn't teach there and feel as if the students were going to get what they were supposed to get. I'd been feeling that way for a little while for a number of reasons, but that episode was really it for me; I just thought it was ridiculous. I know that there are probably a lot of people around this area who would disagree with me, and I respect their opinion, but it was how I felt and still do feel about the issue.

Before I left White House, Mary and I had checked out Pope John Paul II (JPII, as it's known locally), which is a Catholic School in Hendersonville, for Tyler. He was getting old enough for us to be planning about where to go to high school, and JPII was definitely on the radar. One of the people in the music program at JPII told me there was an opening in another Catholic school in Gallatin, Tennessee, called St. John Vianney a brand new school at the time, that needed a music teacher. "You should go by and check it out," they said.

So I did. Sister Louise Busby, who was a nun from Ohio, was the person interviewing folks. We arranged to meet and I had a nice interview with her. At the end she said, "I just want one more thing from you, I would like you to play something for me."

I said, "Well I don't have my guitar." Now, I don't know if you notice about Catholic nuns but they are very difficult to argue with, and Sister Busby replied: "Yes, but I know you play the keyboards and we have a piano here." So I had to agree and

I said that I probably did know how to play a little bit. "I could probably play you something I've written," I said, and she said, "That sounds great!"

We went down to the music room and, sure enough, they had a piano in there so I sat down and played her one of my tunes. I got about two-thirds of the way through and she said: "Yeah you got it." That's exactly how she said it. So I asked, "What do you mean?" and the good Sister said, "I think you'll do just fine at this."

Once you aren't arguing with her anymore, when you get a nun on your side it kind of feels like a sign from God. I thought I was pretty set. But before the beginning of the academic year, this weird thing happened where Sister Busby and most of the rest of the staff were let go, so of course they had to re-staff. As a result, I ended up coming in as a new teacher with a whole bunch of other new teachers and a bunch of new nuns, which was really a strange situation!

I stayed there for several years. I started the music program at St. John Vianney from nothing, and built it up. I feel that this was another part of my life following the stroke where God redeemed me. I'd been so awful at student teaching in college that I'd had to promise never to teach in exchange for getting my degree. So nobody was more pleasantly surprised than I was to win the Wal-Mart teacher of the year at St. John Vianney, for my development of the music program.

Now, I had no ambition for that to happen. It wasn't something I planned or set out to do. I remain so thankful that I got an opportunity to teach those children. I really believe that it helped me to overcome the deficiencies from my stroke. It was possibly the best rehab I could have ever had, because

I had to teach those children the very basics and rudiments of music. Teaching them both the theory and the practical stuff was how I finally taught myself how to really play again. I had to look at my books again. I had to look everything up so that I could teach the kids! Going back to my own music books, and getting myself far enough along to teach, made me a better musician; even better, in some ways, than I had been before the stroke.

From an emotional level too, when you teach something as joyful as music, especially to kids, it's hard to remain unhappy. I truly believe that if everyone had the chance to learn and play a musical instrument to the level of his or her ability the world would be a better place. I further believe that the shifts in funding priorities and curriculum planning that has devalued public school music education is an unhealthy thing for our country's future.

Those years spent teaching, in a school that was intentionally aware of God as part of whom they were, and encouraged God in the lives of the children in their care, was very healing for me. The general wellbeing and happiness of the children was infectious, in a really good way. All that helped lift me out of my funk that came from not remembering how to play.

To that point in my life, having been raised as a Presbyterian, I'd never really been associated with Catholics. Like many Protestants, I really didn't have a very good opinion of Catholics, because I didn't understand what being Catholic really was.

There was also a lot of bad press surrounding the Catholic Church in those days, because of all the horrible things that some priests had been doing to children in their parishes and the cover-up that some misguided church leaders encouraged.

Given all of that, I went into teaching at a Catholic institution with a negative bias, but when I got there the first person I talked with was the priest called Father Choby, who had told me I'd have to audition for Dr. Busby.

The more that I taught there, however, the more I felt enriched by the rituals of the Catholic Church. The ceremony, the symbolism, the Eucharistic feast, pretty much everything that goes with it, somehow provided the meaning in the real world that I suppose may have been missing for me previously.

All I can say is that it really enriched my life. As I was still coming back from that stroke at a number of levels it was possible that I was more of an empty slate once again. Although I was a teacher, I was also as a child. I think the joining of my inner knowledge and faith that God would allow me to come back, combined with this rich tapestry of history and worship ritual, gave me a path that I didn't have before.

You can probably see where this is heading: I became a Catholic myself. I converted, because Father Choby (who eventually became a bishop) took me under his wing, and became an important spiritual mentor to me. To this day, I have never met a man as spiritual as he was. I really wanted to share this book with him, but he died in 2017, before it was finished.

Anyhow, I went through the Rite of Christian Initiation of Adults (RCIA) and became a devout Catholic. Today, though I still enjoy mass at the Catholic Church, I really consider myself a "Christ follower." Denominations to me can be, and are, unfortunately used as divisions among believers. I believe that Christ wants his people to love one another. Along with daily bible reading and prayer, I try to follow that core message of compassion for others.

I'd had my stroke-like event in January 1997, and by 2007 I was increasingly happy in several areas of my life. I was awakening again to my music and God's purpose for me. Unfortunately, my marriage to Mary wasn't going too well. We ended up getting a divorce, which I initiated, at least on paper. This was because in 2007 I discovered my wife Mary, like Denise before her, was having an affair.

I still tried to keep our marriage together, because I thought it would be better for my kids (at least until they were all graduated from High School), no matter how miserable my personal feelings might have been. But Mary had other ideas, so I started divorce proceedings against her.

There are forces of light and darkness in the universe. Whether you call the Dark the devil, or some other name, it does exist, and it does try to hold us back and fight against us, especially if we have re-framed our journey to try and live in accordance with God, the creator of Light. Because I had intentionally positioned myself as someone now trying to do God's will, I think the dark was not happy.

God doesn't abandon you when the chips are down. He often sends angels to help you out. During what would become a long drawn out legal battle, I prayed more than I ever have in my life. One scripture I prayed was from Psalms, chapter 37, verses 27 and 28: "Turn from evil and do good, that you may be settled forever. For the Lord loves justice and does not abandon the faithful."

Sister Martha Ann was certainly one of many angels sent to me to lend a helping hand. She was the principal at St. John Vianney from the moment I discovered Mary's affair, and my family began to be ripped apart. Sister gave me some great counseling in her office on a few occasions and gave me her handmade rosary, made from rosewood, that she had carried for years, to give me comfort. I still carry that rosary in my pocket to this day, and am very thankful for her help during a most difficult time.

After the divorce, I had no desire to ever be in a relationship again. I was telling folks who would ask if I would ever date again that, I've got someone with beautiful curves, a slender neck with beautiful hair, who only talks when I want her too, and makes me feel good every time I hold her. I was of course, talking about my guitar! However God had another plan that would lead me to meet Shannon, the lady who would become the love of my life.

Shannon was teaching at Reagan and Makenzy's school. Reagan, who was in 3rd grade at the time, had brought me in there one day, for one of those things where your kid shows off what you do for a living. I was in there playing music and having a great time. I recall being very happy that day. I also met Shannon. I asked Shannon out to dinner and was pleased, she said yes. We were supposed to go out in February, but I had to postpone the date because of a kidney stone. We rescheduled for May of 2010, the night before the Great Flood of Nashville. We both really enjoyed each other's company, having ate dinner, followed by a walk around the block, where The Ryman Auditorium is located, with much conversation. Later that night we went to Mike's Ice-Cream and got a couple of ice-cream cones. I mention Mike's Ice-Cream because I took Shannon back about a year later, where I sang one of our favorite songs to her, "Hey There Delilah," but changed the last lyric to: "Will you marry me?" she of course said Yes!

Shannon loves Christ and was raised of the Baptist persuasion. We found a local congregation together. I now even play guitar in that Baptist Church (Grace Baptist Church)! Playing guitar in church has finally evolved from something I felt very awkward doing, becoming a beautiful act of worship.

It helps that I really like the pastor there (Pastor Steve Freeman, or as I like to call him, "Preacher Man"). Pastor Steve is a good shepherd and gave me and my family amazing support during some very difficult times. He is another one of those angels whom God placed in my life. The Assistant Pastor at Grace Baptist Church, Johnny McCartney, is also another angel whom God allowed to show up at just the perfect time to defend me during the times of great personal difficulty in the aftermath of my second divorce.

Johnny has the wisdom to discern truth from fiction, and without really knowing me very well trusted his instinct, and possibly God's nudge to protect me. I have many great friends and supporters in the congregation at GBC, and am thankful for them. Though I still feel most at home in the Catholic Church, I think it's important to recognize the amazing amount of great things that are done in the name of Christ by his followers, no matter what labels they affix to themselves.

Chapter 7

STROKED BY GOD
I Got the Music in Me

God is indeed great, and especially once I'd had the
opportunity to teach music to children and relearn music
as a child would once again, His music kept coming back
to me.

By 2004, nearly seven years after the stroke, I had regained a
level of musical ability where I was able to release an album
of nine original tunes, and one Gospel cover: *I'll Fly Away.*
Although I recorded the material mostly in 2004, I didn't
release it until 2006, largely because I also mixed and mastered
all of it myself, and juggling that between teaching and carpet
cleaning was hard to do. The name of that album is *My Grass
is Blue*, in homage to its bluegrass influence. I released it under
the pseudonym of Dr. Johnny Feelgood, a persona I created,
that was loosely based on Howard Hessemann's character
"Johnny Fever," from that great TV show *WKRP in Cincinnati.*
I created my own company, registered as Johnny Jingles Music,
to publish the album, and flow all of my music through this
company today.

In 2007, I composed a song called *My Sweet Child*. I wrote that song for a purpose. It was Thanksgiving eve, the first time during the whole divorce mess that my children wouldn't be with me. In addition, a student of mine at St. John Vianney had cancer and a fellow teacher had a son being deployed to Afghanistan. All those things were weighing heavy on me when I wrote *My Sweet Child*. I wrote it very quickly, probably in about ten minutes, and straight from the heart. It was one of those moments when God clearly guided my mind and my heart to make music that would serve His purpose.

Although I was getting healthier and healthier the stress around all of the mess going on in my personal life held me back from writing much. It certainly stopped me from recording and mixing my material. One exception to this is a fun little instrumental tune I wrote called *The Mosquito*, which evokes the noise of a mosquito hovering around. After the divorce was over, I married my blessing, Shannon Wright, in 2011. We live very happily together in my house in Springfield, Tennessee.

Sadly, 2011 was also the year that I was let go from my teaching position. In the aftermath of the financial meltdown of 2008-2009, the budgets of almost every kind of institution took a hit, including those of private schools, and music became a low priority on the budgetary totem pole. I see this happening everywhere today in our country's school system, and, once again, I think it is a huge mistake. There are all sorts of scientific studies that show the benefits of learning music in a child's intellectual development, and the therapeutic benefits of learning and playing music to patients with various cognitive impairments, such as alzheimer's disease, and, yes, stroke survivors.

By now I'd learned to see God's hand in everything to do with my life, and once the opportunity to teach came to an end, I realized I was by now a better musician technically than I had been before my stroke!

I began writing music more intentionally again and also covering other tunes by developing new arrangements for them. In November 2015, I released an instrumental cover album called *My Heaven is Blue*, which is nearly all guitar, and which includes tracks such as *Amazing Grace*, *Jesus Loves Me*, and *We Three Kings*. Given the advances in technology now available to musicians, I release my music as an independent artist through a great platform called CDBaby, which releases many musicians from the iron hand of the record labels.

Around this time, I also began playing more frequently in public, not just at Grace Baptist Church, but at other churches and venues as well. One day after I had started doing this, a pastor from South Carolina, who had studied under the pastor at our church, came to pay his mentor a visit. It turned out that he had lost one of his daughters to illness when she was only 9 years old. I asked him if I could play a song for him. He said yes, and so I played *My Sweet Child* for him and his family. It was a tough thing to get through emotionally, but he allowed afterwards that the song had a healing quality to it. He encouraged me to share it more widely.

Shortly afterwards, I played at an event in Hendersonville, Tennessee, called Porchfest, which is a musical event that celebrates the kind of music that I literally heard on my porch growing up in Gastonia. I told a joke beforehand, to lighten the mood, then to make sure the audience understood my intention about what I was going to play for them, I told a story of a "little boy" who grew up in the North Carolina hills, and his journey of following his dream to Nashville, becoming a utility musician, and of his success in the music industry, before suffering a stroke which robbed him of his ability to play.

Then I shared how this "little boy," now a man, was redeemed by God, and how God restored this man's ability to play, and that how, today, he is a better musician than he ever was. Then I told them I was that little boy, now the man they saw before them. Then I played *My Sweet Child* for them, and, of course, it was very moving. People love the redemptive power of both stories, and many have suggested I should write a book about it all, which is the main reason you are now reading the book you have in your hands.

I'd probably describe myself today as the modern equivalent of a traveling minstrel. I may never make a lot of money from my music, but it is mine, or at least it is God's music flowing through me. No record label can ever refuse to sign me because I "didn't sell enough units" or "don't have a large enough social media following." My old ideas of what constituted "success" in music have been completely stood on their head, transformed, as my life was transformed, by the unequivocal intention of God in my life.

It was only recently that I discovered what had likely happened to me back in 1997, through the help of an excellent physician, who possesses the ability to clearly relate to lay people what is happening, or what has happened to them. She agreed that the drug I was put on, the high-dose, slow-release drug called Cardizem-SR, may have helped cause the strange medical disaster that I experienced. Finally, she was also able to share with me the most likely explanation for what happened: This drug lowers blood pressure by opening up the blood vessels in your body, and also by slowing your heart rate. When used properly, it is a very good and effective medication. But the SR (Slow Release) effect lasts for a long time. When a physician first prescribes it, you should start with a lower dose and work your way up gradually, to make sure you aren't getting too much right off the bat.

Instead, my very first dose was a pretty high one. I was told to take it at bedtime. When I went to sleep that night, my blood vessels opened up, but they stayed too open for too long. Normally, your heart compensates for this happening by beating faster, but my heart couldn't accommodate in this way, due to the heart-rate-lowering effect of the medicine. As a result of all this, maybe what happened to me is that my blood pressure was too low, and my heartbeat too slow, for enough oxygen to get to my brain. Again, I don't know for sure if this is what actually happened to me, but it's the only explanation I've heard that has ever made any sense.

Because this was a more or less "global" effect, I didn't have the "one-side-of-the-body" effect you see in people who have had a typical stroke. But it can explain why my intelligence was so impaired while my physical function came back pretty quickly. That my brain rewired at all is a miracle due to God, possibly to my long musical training and experience, and to the intricacies of learning music all over again.

God doesn't just give life. He gives it more abundantly. I've already mentioned that I'm a better musician than I ever was even before the "stroke." Over time, the rewiring, and re-programming, of the neural pathways in my brain took another, even more miraculous turn. While I was cleaning carpets for a living, I began to be very dissatisfied with the cleaning solvents and solutions I could find on the market. They were often toxic, usually bad for the environment, and worst of all, just didn't work on any difficult stains!

I pondered this problem a lot, until one day the answer just came into my head all at once. Although I never had any education in chemistry, or anything like that, one day I suddenly received this full-blown insight about how to concoct an environmentally-friendly, stable, and effective solution for getting stains out of carpets. I began using it with my carpet-cleaning clients, to rave reviews.

Finally, in 2017 I took the financial plunge to trademark the solution, which I call Jingle Clean®, after my music label, Johnny Jingles Music Group. As it happened, I had been contemplating two different names for my stain remover: Jingle Clean® and Bubble Clean. I had been asking customers and friends which name they liked best and without exception Jingle Clean® was the first choice. My trademark attorney John Prince, who had convinced me to launch Jingle Clean® texted me a photo of his blue crushed-velvet sofa and chair. His dog had eaten a laundry detergent pod and had gotten really sick, defecating bloody stools and vomiting all over his furniture. John asked if I thought Jingle Clean® could clean it. I simply said, "I don't know, let's try."

I went to John's home and cleaned the furniture with Jingle Clean® and you could not tell it had ever been dirty! Both John and I were astonished, after which John said: "Man that JC stuff is amazing!" I immediately felt a cold chill hit me like a ton of bricks, JC: Jesus Christ! What an affirmation to receive for a product God inspired. Truly, everything happens for a reason!

I manufactured the first commercial batch of Jingle Clean® in my home, using over-stock bottles which I had ordered online. Since then, I've found an affordable third-party manufacturing option, very close to home, and have been able to gear up production. Jingle Clean® has been available online for some time, and as you can imagine, I'm leveraging my old contacts at

Kroger's to see if I can't get representation in their stores, at least locally!

It's my hope that Jingle Clean® will provide enough financial security against the day when I can't haul around heavy carpet cleaning equipment anymore, and also serve to finance the recording, mixing, and mastering of my music, so I don't have to do all of that myself, which in turn should hopefully mean that I'm able to get more of my own music, the music that God wants me to compose and produce, out to the world. One thing I do know for sure: I'll never manage somebody else's music again, because a really big "Somebody Else" wants me to manage His music for Him!

Jingle Clean® is not the only invention I've been inspired to share with the world. More are on their way, as God continues to place these scientific insights into a brain with no scientific training! I love these miracles, and love that God has asked me to be his vessel for sharing them with the world. But no miracles have moved me as much as that day I first heard, really heard, those birds in the trees, and first felt, really felt, that breeze on my face, except perhaps for the day I surrendered, really surrendered, to God's will for my life.

I hope my story will help you also discover how amazing God can be, if you just slow down enough to listen to the birds, feel the breeze across your face, and accept His will for your life. I could wish nothing better for you, because then you too will know what it's like to be...

Stroked by God
John Bumgardner and Paul Deepan
Tennessee, 2018

John Bumgardner

is a virtuoso guitarist, multi-instrument musician, and singer-songwriter, originally from Gastonia, North Carolina. His first major success came when he moved to Nashville, Tennessee and became a guitar player and manager for Paulette Carlson, (founding member of *Highway 101*.)

But, nearing the height of his career in the music industry, John suffered a devastating medical event with many symptoms of a stroke. This event seriously affected his dexterity and memory to the point he could no longer play his instruments.

John's unshakable faith sustained him on a two-decade path to recovery. Through God's grace, John has not only recovered his ability to play music. He now plays better than he ever did. In addition, John has released his own album, *My Heaven is Blue*, and continues to write and perform music in the Nashville area.

Although he received no formal training in science, John is also the inventor of Jingle Clean®, an environmentally-friendly and pet-safe cleaner which can be used to treat stains on carpets and many other fabrics. John again credits God with intuitively granting him the knowledge to create Jingle Clean.

In thanksgiving for the way God has redeemed him, John often shares his story from the stage when he performs. Many folks have encouraged him to write a book about his journey.

Stroked by God is the poignant, funny, and inspirational story of John's rise within the music business, his catastrophic stroke-like event, and the power of God's healing and redemption.

By sharing his story, John hopes that you too will be...
Stroked by God.

John's music can be found at johnnyjingles.com

Jingle Clean® can be found at jingleclean.com or on Amazon

Paul Deepan

was born in Port-of-Spain, Trinidad, and has lived for extended periods in Trinidad, England, Canada, and the United States. He expended a large portion of his earlier life accumulating university degrees in the life sciences and business administration. He is currently a recovering pharmaceutical industry executive and writing addict.

Paul is the author of the award-winning fantasy novel, *The Fruit of the Dendragon Tree*, and co-author (with Rich Redmond, drummer for country superstar Jason Aldean) of the Amazon bestseller *The CRASH! Course for Success*.

Paul has also written and produced several songs, including the collaboration with John Bumgardner, his co-author on *Stroked by God*, called *Find Your Life*, featuring Rich Redmond on the drums.

When not pursuing his own creative interests, Paul ghostwrites and edits books for a diverse set of clients that have included business leaders, musicians, and athletes. *Stroked by God* is his fourth such collaboration to be published.

Paul currently resides near Nashville, Tennessee, with his wife Lori and a menagerie of rescue animals.